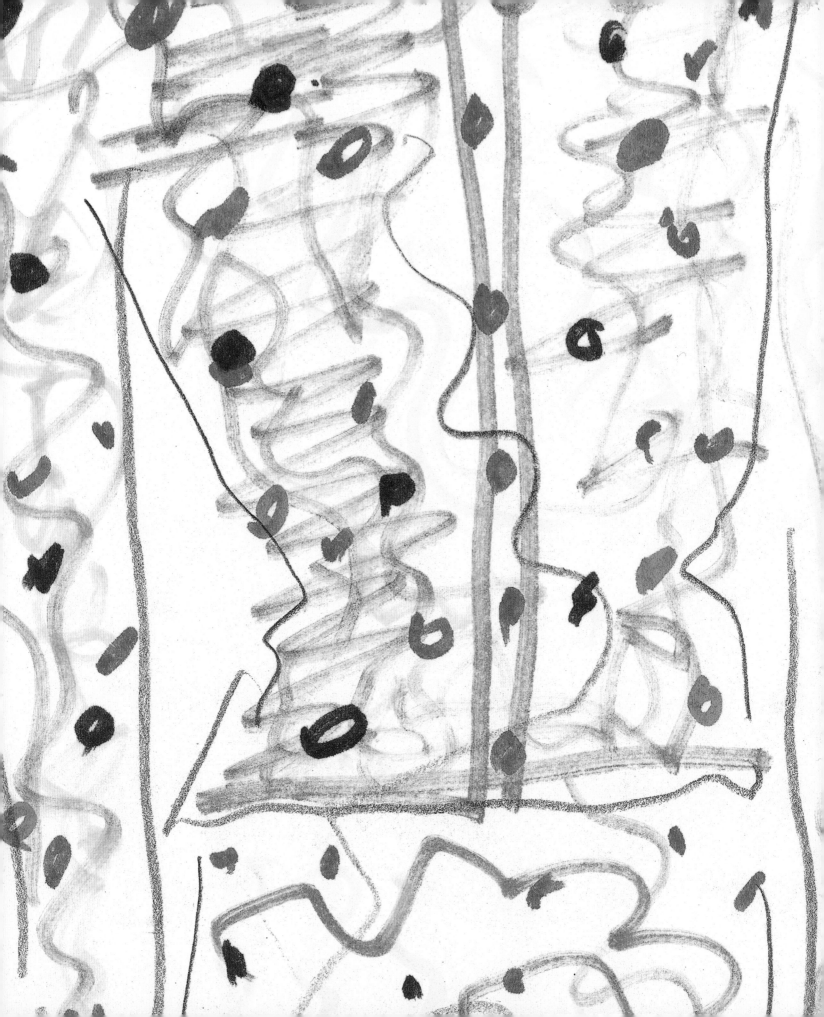

YVES SAINT LAURENT STYLE STYLE STYLE

ABRAMS, NEW YORK

CONTENTS

11 YVES SAINT LAURENT
12 RETROSPECTIVE 1962–2002
15 A MIRROR TO HIS TIME
20 THE SAINT LAURENT STYLE

28 AT THE PENCIL POINT
31 STYLE IN MOVEMENT
40 THE BODY REVEALED
48 REDEFINING THE SILHOUETTE

52 THE YVES SAINT LAURENT REVOLUTION
55 MASCULINE-FEMININE
74 AN AMBIGUOUS ATTRACTION
84 FUNDAMENTALS FOR THE EVENING

94 THE PALETTE
97 MOROCCO
104 IMAGINARY VOYAGES
140 COLORS AND TEXTURES
150 GEOMETRY

158 LYRICAL SOURCES
161 OVER TIME
168 DIALOGUE WITH ART
192 LITERATURE
200 GLAMOUR
208 ANIMALS
218 FLORA

238 BIOGRAPHY

246 APPENDIXES
248 CHRONOLOGICAL INDEX OF DESIGNS
249 HAUTE COUTURE SUPPLIERS

YVES SAINT LAURENT

When Yves Saint Laurent decided to end his career in 2002, we immediately started the plan to create a foundation. Thus began the Fondation Pierre Bergé–Yves Saint Laurent, fundamentally aiming to preserve the five thousand items of clothing designed by Yves Saint Laurent, as well as more than fifteen thousand drawings, sketches, and miscellaneous items.

The foundation is principally responsible for spreading the work of Yves Saint Laurent through exhibitions and cultural and educational events. We are, therefore, particularly delighted about the retrospective in Montreal in summer of 2008 and in San Francisco in fall of 2008. The first Yves Saint Laurent exhibition was held in 1983 at the Metropolitan Museum of Art in New York, at the instigation of Diana Vreeland. Twenty-five years later, we are honored to return to North America. This retrospective displays the huge range of the work of our creative designer. We shall see how—and with what panache—he became the successor to Christian Dior and how, over the years, he imposed his own style. Let's say it again: Fashion changes, but style remains. Yves Saint Laurent's style is recognizable to everyone. It takes its root in its respect for women and their bodies. Never was a garment created just to satisfy a whim; all of them were placed in the service of women.

It has often been said that Chanel liberated women. That's true. Years later, Saint Laurent would give them power. As we all know, power lies in the hands of men. Hence, taking inspiration from masculine dress—by sliding masculine shoulders onto those of women, dressing them in tuxedos, reefer jackets, blazers, sport coats, and trench coats—Saint Laurent, in his own way, transferred power to women. He strived socially, much more than others, for equality of the sexes and for the acknowledgment of the modern woman, not just as an object, but as someone who contributes to society and asserts her own confidence.

In this way, the work of Yves Saint Laurent goes much further than that of a fashion designer. He extended the realm of aesthetics to embrace social issues, using in a certain way the approach of a moralist. This retrospective should be viewed in this perspective. Of course, Saint Laurent wanted women to be beautiful and, as much as anyone else—and with more talent—he glorified them, but primarily he reassured them, gave them self-confidence, enabled them to confront everyday life and, above all, allowed them to see their own selves.

Pierre Bergé

RETROSPECTIVE 1962–2002

The Montreal Museum of Fine Art and the Fine Arts Museums of San Francisco are proud to collaborate with the Fondation Pierre Bergé–Yves Saint Laurent to bring the first complete retrospective of Yves Saint Laurent's work to North America. Twenty-five years have passed since his groundbreaking retrospective opened in 1983 at the Metropolitan Museum of Art's Costume Institute in New York. Yves Saint Laurent remains the most influential fashion designer of the second half of the twentieth century, famed for having revolutionized the haute couture tradition and developed a new wardrobe for the modern, emancipated woman during the heady days of the 1960s. Throughout his forty-year career, he continued to push the boundaries of sartorial design—merging the worlds of fashion and art. A classicist—fond of discipline—as well as a provocateur, Yves Saint Laurent used his extensive artistic vocabulary to quote from the streets of Paris, London, or New York as freely as he drew inspiration from the writings of Shakespeare, Cocteau, or Proust, or the paintings of Matisse, Picasso, and Mondrian.

A look at Saint Laurent's entire career—from the first collection he produced after founding his own fashion house in 1962 to his final show in 2002—provides the opportunity to reveal his creative approach. Throughout his work, Saint Laurent continuously explored, reinterpreted, and perfected several tendencies. Working within the Modernist tradition, he created timeless, universal principles of dress—the Yves Saint Laurent standards—which extended beyond the trench coat and tuxedo to his use of color, line, and imagery. This exhibition and its catalog thematically display the clothing to show how his core principles evolved. Many of the one hundred and sixty pieces have never been seen in a museum context.

The exhibition was developed in three cities around the world—Paris, Montreal, and San Francisco—involving an international team of curators who combined their respective expertise and cultural sensibilities. First and foremost, the museums and curatorial team wish to thank Yves Saint Laurent and Pierre Bergé, for their enthusiasm and willingness to see the artist's output presented through this project. We are grateful to French fashion historian and curator Florence Müller, who shared her passion for, and extensive knowledge of, fashion and French couture with Diane Charbonneau, Curator of Contemporary Decorative Arts at the Montreal Museum of Fine Arts, and Jill D'Alessandro, Associate Curator of the Caroline and H. McCoy Jones Department of Textile Arts at the Fine Arts Museums of San Francisco. Together they have produced a comprehensive survey of Yves Saint Laurent's vision and his unique and vibrant talent.

A number of individuals participated in making this project possible. Baroness Hélène de Ludinghausen, director of the Yves Saint Laurent haute couture salons for more than thirty years, first opened doors to new opportunities some years ago when she introduced Yves Saint Laurent and Pierre Bergé to John E. Buchanan, Jr. We thank the staff at the Fondation Pierre Bergé–Yves Saint Laurent, who graciously made the foundation's archives available to the curators and allowed them to research Yves Saint Laurent's oeuvre from a different viewpoint. They were fortunate enough to work with Dominique Deroche, who has presided over the fashion house for more than forty years, and Robin Fournier-Bergmann, who facilitated the trips through the archives by providing his reliable assistance. Selecting one hundred and sixty accessorized models from a collection of five thousand costumes and more than fifteen thousand accessories was a challenging undertaking, but it turned into a treasure hunt with the help of Laurence Neveu and Frédéric Verdure. The dedication and patience of Mireille Prulhière during this process also deserves special mention. The project ran smoothly from beginning to end thanks to the organizational skills of Sophie Aurand. We are also grateful to the rest of the staff of the foundation who contributed their efforts to this exhibition and its accompanying publication. Nathalie Crinière of Agence NC, Paris, is responsible for the inspiring presentation of Yves Saint Laurent's models. But most importantly, all of them generously shared their knowledge and passion for Yves Saint Laurent's legacy.

This lavishly illustrated publication, which accompanies the exhibition, was produced in French by Éditions de La Martinière, Paris, and in English by Abrams, New York, under the skillful art direction of Philippe Appeloig. It stands out from previous publications on the subject of Yves Saint Laurent by featuring unpublished models, detailed captions, as well as an illustrated chronology. Alexandre Guirkinger, who brought great sensitivity to the photographic interpretation of models, took photographs especially for this publication. We are also pleased to express our appreciation to the authors, Florence Müller and Hamish Bowles, who provided us with insightful and enlightened texts.

We hope that this unique exhibition will have an everlasting impact on our audiences. Known for the originality and diversity of its exhibition program, the Montreal Museum of Fine Arts inspires to attract a diverse public by presenting thought-provoking shows developed from a wide range of inspirations. This complete retrospective of Yves Saint Laurent falls within this realm, while contributing to the creative activities produced by the community of designers, local consultants, and fashion firms that have made Montreal a world-class fashion center.

For the Fine Arts Museums of San Francisco, women's costume and, more specifically, French haute couture holds a special place within the voluminous collections of the Caroline and H. McCoy Jones Department of Textile Arts. These collections have grown over the years thanks to donations from the generous women of San Francisco. If museum collections reflect the artistic and cultural currents of their cities, then San Francisco belongs to Yves Saint Laurent. No other designer is more widely represented in the collections than him, with more than one hundred and fifty examples of his costumes. Yves Saint Laurent's genius speaks to each and every woman, allowing her to express her own individuality.

On behalf of both the Montreal Museum of Art and the Fine Arts Museums of San Francisco, we would like to acknowledge the commitment of the museum staffs who contributed to the success of this exhibition. Finally, we are grateful for the great opportunity provided by these two North American museums that have valued collaboration and have worked on such a discerning exhibition.

Nathalie Bondil Director, Montreal Museum of Art

John E. Buchanan, Jr. Director of Museums, Fine Arts Museums of San Francisco

A MIRROR TO HIS TIME

Through six decades of momentous and immeasurable change, Yves Saint Laurent held a mirror up to his times. From the hothouse atmosphere of Christian Dior's pearl gray salons to the iconoclasm of the Punk street, Saint Laurent captured the zeitgeist with uncanny acuity; his work suggesting in turns the designer as clairvoyant and as keeper of the sacred flame of a barely remembered era of elegance. "His life is a legend," wrote Bernard-Henri Lévy in 1986, "His name is an empire." More than two decades later, Saint Laurent's design legacy of innovation and tradition, of impeccable understatement and startling modernity, of the bravura grand gesture and the whispering detail, ensures his preeminence in fashion's pantheon.

In March 1957, *Time* magazine featured Christian Dior on its cover, wielding a pair of vast dressmaker's scissors. "In an epoch as somber as ours," Dior declared, "luxury must be defended inch by inch." In one of the magazine's candid photographs, Dior and his *équipe* scrutinize the effect of a scarlet faille evening coat over a pale linen dress. The ordered chaos of the studio, with its thickets of toiles and hat forms, its bolts of fabrics, and its velvet and satin trays of costume jewelry, belies the intensity of the process. "We are placed under the sign of the ephemeral," Dior explained, "Rigorous construction, precision of cut, quality of execution alone separate us from the travesty of fancy dress."

Staring intently into the studio's mirrored wall at the mannequin's reflected form is the lithe, bespectacled figure of the youthful Yves Mathieu Saint Laurent, by then the house's quietly acknowledged dauphin. A year later, following Christian Dior's untimely death, this same shy, but steely young man—astonishingly only twenty-one—was to be thrust into the limelight, summoned to the balcony of Dior's avenue Montaigne palace of haute couture to accept the accolades of the fashion world for his debut collection for the house. For several seasons Saint Laurent's designs had been passing more or less unaltered through the studio and into the collections. For instance in Richard Avedon's iconic image of Dovima, posing between prancing elephants, the dress she wears—"Soirée de Paris," from the Fall–Winter 1955 collection, a sheath of black velvet swathed under the bust with ivory duchesse satin, which cascades into a dramatic sideswept floating panel—was a pure Saint Laurent creation (it subsequently would be commissioned by Marlene Dietrich). Saint Laurent was thus acutely sensitive to the collaborative Dior process, which involved the interventions of what Cecil Beaton called "the three fates," Madame Raymonde Zehnacker, who oversaw the studio (a role that Anne-Marie Munoz-Yague would assume in Saint Laurent's own house); Madame Marguerite Carré, the technical genius who had followed Dior from Lucien Lelong; and the inscrutable Mitzah Bricard, ostensibly the milliner, but essentially the designer's muse who would tweak and accessorize every outfit to lend it the intangible panache that marked it as a Dior original. Before the War, Captain Molyneux had relied on Bricard's sure eye and orchidaceous elegance to add the finishing flourishes to his self-effacing clothes, and Dior himself would consider her invaluable. "She was his dancer and courtesan," remembered Alexander Liberman. "With her rustling silks, her poses, her pearls, and her points of view on everything and nothing, she was feminine seduction incarnate."

Each season, Christian Dior and his *équipe* would reinvent and finesse the best sellers of the previous season for the conservative clients, but leaven the collection with a handful of dramatic designs that would emphatically reinforce the message and the new statement "line" of the season, which would appeal to the fashion journalists, international department and specialty store buyers, as well as the house's more adventurous patrons. For his debut, Saint Laurent subtly referenced Dior's A-line, of Spring–Summer 1955. (When Saint Laurent had presented in 1954 a portfolio of his work to Michel de Brunhoff, *French Vogue*'s director, it was partly the uncanny resemblance of the young man's fashion designs to those in the new A-Line collection, which Dior had yet to unveil—but had already presented to de Brunhoff—that led the director to present the seventeen-year-old youth to Christian Dior, who hired him on the spot.)

It was a characteristically subtle, but instinctive Saint Laurent gesture to have grounded his first collection in the house's history, but also to have added an entirely new dimension of youthful lightheartedness. This was literally expressed in the buoyant, airy silhouette, which appeared to float, unencumbered, from the body (in reality, the *Trapeze* garments are artfully constructed over a base of elaborately structured and corseted underpinnings). The collection was a triumph. The newspaper sellers shouted, "Saint Laurent has saved France!" *Vogue* reported of the exhilarating reception that the collection received: "The joy and relief were terrific—people cried, laughed, clapped, and shook hands." "The Saint Laurent phenomenon succeeds to the Christian Dior phenomenon," wrote *French Vogue*. But Saint Laurent's five subsequent Dior collections were perceived by the establishment to have injected a little too much youth for the bourgeois clientele, particularly in his Fall–Winter 1959 collection with its poufed skirts cinched at the knee and his prophetic Fall–Winter 1960 collection, which brought existentialist panda-eyed Mod style, complete with hand-knit turtlenecks and black crocodile biker-boy blousons, to Dior's rarefied salons. Saint Laurent was ultimately offered up for the dreaded army draft from which he had been so carefully protected, while Marc Bohan assumed the design direction of Dior, pleasing clients with the uncomplicated prettiness and elegant conservatism of his work.

Saint Laurent meanwhile, with the indomitable Pierre Bergé at his side, rose from the ashes of the Dior debacle and the breakdown that followed his army career to create a house of his own in a pale and airy townhouse on rue Spontini in Passy, far from the café society bustle of the avenue Montaigne. The fashionable world was crowded into its small salons for the first collection, on January 29, 1962, among them Princess Lee Radziwill, Jacqueline Kennedy's impeccably chic sister; the flamboyant beauty impresario Helena Rubinstein (in a Peruvian bowler hat); celebrity dancer Zizi Jeanmaire; and society hostesses the Vicomtesse Jacqueline de Ribes and Aileen Plunkett (in cat's-eye sunglasses). For the press—anticipating perhaps the fashion drama that so unsettled the Dior establishment—Saint Laurent's debut was somewhat underwhelming. "The collection surprised only by its sobriety," wrote the *London Sunday Times*'s Ernestine Carter. "Saint Laurent broke no new ground in design," noted *Vogue*, ". . . but there were beauties that will surely be seen at elegant parties in New York, Paris, London, Rome— over and over again." *Life* magazine, however, astutely noted that the collection included the best group of suits since Chanel. At the time, Saint Laurent told *Corriere della Sera*'s Dino Buzzi that he wasn't working to get his name in the press, but instead to create clothes that all women could wear. In 1974, he told *British Vogue*'s Polly Devlin, "I don't try to make revolutionary clothes every time, I don't try to be sensational but . . . I'm not static in my thinking or emotions or my designing."

Saint Laurent's debut may have been tentative and calculatedly client friendly, but among the tiered shantung tunic ensembles and gently fitted suits, there were harbingers of the fireworks to come. Maharajah tunics, whimsical turbans, and babushka headscarf hats suggested the magical voyages that the designer would transport his clients on—to Morocco, Spain, Russia, China, Africa—through the subsequent decades, while a gold-buttoned naval caban, worn over pale trousers and with Moroccan babouches, presaged the borrowings from a man's wardrobe that would eventually transform the way women dressed. Saint Laurent's elegant restraint had the desired effect. "The next day, there was a rush of international personalities ordering six or seven costumes at a clip," noted *Vogue*. In the vanguard was the supremely elegant Patricia Lopez-Wilshaw, embodiment of mid-century style and patron of Charles James, Balenciaga, Elsa Schiaparelli et al, whose jet-encrusted evening gown was branded with the typed model number 00001. Like Dior's own mentors Lucien Lelong and Robert Piguet, and Edward Molyneux (whom Dior greatly admired), Saint Laurent was compelled to create clothes that would flatter and seduce women. In 1983, he noted that "if one tries to impose one's own interests, one's own fantasies, ahead of those of women, one ends up with disguises. It means keeping a little distance from the thing you create, pushing it toward others, toward the woman."

He worked by draping toiles and fabrics on the models (chosen for their personalities and verve as much as their looks and figures), who would often stimulate his creative process—from the sultry Victoire Doutreleau to the voluptuous Mounia. "I think I attach more importance to the movement of a body than to the way it is dressed," Saint Laurent has said, "Some women can be dressed in a perfectly ordinary way and be very, very elegant and extraordinary, if only by their personalities and their gestures." As his muse, Loulou de la Falaise, uniting the bohemian-aristocratic elegance of her mother Maxime (daughter of the fashionable portraitist Sir Oswald Birley) to a spirit of Anglo-Irish eccentricity (she was married to the Knight of Glin) and of Swinging London iconoclasm, brought together elements that had a profound effect on Saint Laurent's oeuvre. But there were other influences shaping his vision of fashion. While some haute couture designers of his generation were attempting to capture the zeitgeist of the times with futuristic experiments and older hands were resisting radical change altogether, Saint Laurent seems to have had a keener understanding of the dramatically changing times. Pop and Op Art imagery was to impact the form and decoration of Saint Laurent's clothes, notably in his Fall–Winter 1965 collection with its color-block Mondrian–inspired pieces and his Spring–Summer 1966 collection with its playful Warholian Pop motifs. In 1964, *Vogue* found him "a more glorious success than ever, an established artist working at the peak of his powers."

But other developments would define Saint Laurent as the designer of the moment. His discovery of Morocco, where he acquired his first house, in Marrakech—*El Hanch* (the Serpent)—in 1968, introduced a whole new color palette into his work. The safe Molyneux grays and navies, the Parisian taupes and beiges, the melting pastels, and the clear, strong colors that were a legacy of Dior ceded to brilliant hues and startlingly unexpected combinations that soon established the designer as the master colorist of his generation. In 1966, Saint Laurent opened the first of his Rive Gauche boutiques, deftly translating his design talents to the very different discipline of the ready-to-wear. In the Fall-Winter collection that same year, he launched "Le Smoking" for women, with pantsuits following in Spring–Summer 1967. With these masterstrokes, Saint Laurent effectively created a contemporary uniform for a woman that was neither futuristic fancy dress nor asexual garb. "A woman dressed as a man must be at the height of her femininity to fight against a costume that isn't hers," Saint Laurent told Joan Juliet Buck in 1983, citing a 1930s image of Marlene Dietrich, dressed in a man-tailored trouser suit, as a defining touchstone for his philosophy.

"I wanted to make a base that would be changeless, for a man and for a woman," he said at the time, "It was absolutely a conscious choice. I've noticed that men were surer of themselves than women, because their clothes don't change . . . while women were a little abandoned, sometimes terrified, by a fashion that was coming in, or fashion that was only for those under thirty. And I rebelled against that, and since then I have tried every year to perfect a classic style, and that's my safe place. I can do all sorts of other things, but I always come back there."

By 1969, the year he showed *Sahariennes* and garbed the Duchess of Windsor in hippie de luxe patchwork, Saint Laurent was being acclaimed as "the activist of the French couture." The remarkable fecundity of Saint Laurent's ideas—what Diana Vreeland described as "a turmoil of imagination"—produced *The Forties Look* collection of Spring–Summer 1971. This collection, controversial as it was at the time, signaled the death-knell for sixties futurism and heralded instead a decade of romantic nostalgia, which would see Saint Laurent evoke in turns the Russia of the Tsars, the glory years of Hollywood, the heroines of Proust, and the Spain of Carmen.

Saint Laurent followed the fireworks of *The Forties* show with a succession of collections that were essays in pragmatic refinement, and subtle reinventions of the elements and leitmotifs that were already his signatures; the immaculately cut pantsuits, the evening tuxedos, the prim *après-midi* dresses, the triumphantly elegant evening gowns. These ineffably client-friendly clothes suggested that he had inherited the mantles of both Chanel and Balenciaga. (In the 1960s, Chanel herself, generally vociferous in her denunciation of fellow designers, had declared Saint Laurent her only worthy successor.) Gerry Dryansky, writing in *Vogue* in 1980, noted that these collections were "like stockpiles of essentials in times of famine." They also suggested the designer's complicity with his technical ateliers: "When I give the ateliers a sketch they can immediately recognize the direction of the fabric," he said, "They can read it like a road map." This low-key elegance was ignited by the brilliance and spectacle of the Fall–Winter 1976 *Russian* collection, which transformed the fashionable silhouette. *The New York Times* called it "revolutionary" and Anthony Burgess (author of *A Clockwork Orange*), noted that "nobody has to swallow the whole, rich draft, nobody could. But you can sip, you can make your own mild cocktail of the ingredients." By the late 1970s, Saint Laurent had retreated from the street, his taste repulsed by the iconoclasm of Punk. "I feel isolated from these kids," he said, "That aesthetic—the leather, the destruction of harmony—is a loser's choice . . . only style counts; style is that safe place."

With this thought as his mantra, Saint Laurent spent much of the ensuing years, until his retirement in 2002, honing, refining, and finessing the iconic silhouettes and leitmotifs that were his alone. His hieratic couture clothes, presented in an atmosphere of stately magnificence in the gilded Troisième Republique salon of the Hotel Intercontinental in Paris, were studies in faultless technique. They gave his pan-generational clients an unparalleled assurance and an insouciant panache—sex appeal without vulgarity, coquetry, and glamour that evoked Yves Saint Laurent's earliest memories of feminine allure.

Hamish Bowles

THE SAINT LAURENT STYLE

The Fondation Pierre Bergé–Yves Saint Laurent is a one-of-a-kind institution. Located in a mansion on the avenue Marceau in Paris, it contains salons, a creative studio, the offices and workshops of the couture house, spaces in which to hold events and exhibitions, as well as archives of major importance for consulting the collections. More than forty years of the history of Yves Saint Laurent creativity can be visited here, stored in the reserves and Compactus storage units filled with five thousand suits (complete ensembles) and also shown in the thematic exhibitions organized by the museum team. But the mansion is much more than just a memory bank. The whole place vibrates to the rhythm of its founders, who continue to animate it with their passion for fashion. From the 1970s, Pierre Bergé and Yves Saint Laurent intuitively realized the importance of transmitting, for the present and future of fashion, the quintessence of the style of this couture house. So they invented the concept of a fashion heritage, which has since gathered pace into a movement. No luxury house today designs new products without drawing inspiration from the elements of the past. This is known as respect for the genetic codes of the brand, interpretations of the DNA of the label. Yet no house, other than the YSL house, possesses collections of such richness, constituted by their creator down the years, season after season. This selection offers a complete vision of the couturier's oeuvre and makes it possible to faithfully retrace all of the moments that mark a life and work dedicated to feminine beauty. It is another fulfillment of Yves Saint Laurent's desire, as stated in *Elle* magazine: "I should like people in a hundred years' time to be studying my dresses, my drawings."[1]

Without waiting that long, the Yves Saint Laurent retrospective offers a glimpse of the comprehensiveness of the designer's work, exemplary in the repercussions it had on contemporary fashion, rich in lessons for the age of creativity. The importance of the collections has made it possible to focus the choices on the fundamentals of the creator's style, comparing his work with the era and retaining examples illustrating the Saint Laurent revolution. When, in his youth, Yves Saint Laurent created the Trapeze line at Christian Dior in 1958, his entry into fashion was hailed as a sensation by the press. Behind this change in garment proportions in 1955, lay the outline of a more radical change in the whole institution of haute couture. It happened at just the right time, when the zeitgeist gave young people a voice. Yves Saint Laurent was also young, like those who used the power of speech on the barricades, such as Françoise Sagan and Bernard Buffet, or the creators of Pop Art. But his revolution did not proceed to demolish the institution he had created. He acted as a relay between the old and the new worlds of fashion, with a foot in one while looking toward the other. That is how he saw himself: "I grew up in an environment that was very attached to tradition. Yet, at the same time, I wanted to change all that, because I was torn between the attraction of the past and the future that urged me forward."[2]

During the course of his career, Yves Saint Laurent created numerous models that have become fashion icons and subjects to be reflected upon by the creators of fashion. The Mondrian model of 1965, one of the first, taught an exemplary lesson: Clothing cannot be seen as sculpture. On the contrary, it is like a mobile, an object in perpetual motion, a flexible structure with multiple facets. In his biography by Laurence Benaïm, the couturier states clearly: "I understood that until then, the world was rigid and that the time had come to make it move." Haute couture before then, as practiced at Christian Dior, offered women a total look, decked out in finery, magnificent, but frozen into poses that were too perfect. The 1960s, which opened with the launch of the house of Yves Saint Laurent, expected something different from fashion. Haute couture was one of the symbols of the bourgeois order against which the younger generation was rebelling: Great Britain began to live according to the rhythm of Swinging London; in San Francisco, in 1967, hippies gathered for the first Human Be-in; in Paris, in May 1968, activist students were busy "doing." Everything was moving to the rhythm of the dance, to the music, and the challenge of the Pop Age. From 1968 onward, Saint Laurent challenged the vision adopted by some of his colleagues, those who approached clothes in the spirit of architects or sculptors, in a manner that was too conceptual: "Couture is not an art, but a craft. That is to say, its starting point and aim is something concrete. The body of a woman, not an abstract idea, is of intrinsic value in itself. A dress is not architecture, it's a house: It is not made to be contemplated but to be lived in, and the woman who lives in it must feel herself beautiful and right in it. Everything else is just craziness." To construct his garments, the young Saint Laurent insisted on a living model, a moving body, not a tailor's dummy: "A garment should live and it will then be put on stage in everyday life, and to be able to do this, I need the body of a woman." Women of outstanding beauty took their places alongside the couturier, who was determined to idealize them: Victoire Doutreleau, Zizi Jeanmaire, Catherine Deneuve, Loulou de La Falaise, Betty Catroux. . . . The mental projection of their idealization is shaped by destiny. It is the moment of creation in its purest form. Marguerite Duras said it in all her poetry: "A woman. She is there. And he, he is here. He draws. And behold the woman, dressed."[3] The couturier always begins by drawing the face of a woman, then her shoulders; in this regard, Saint Laurent explains "A garment is held on by its shoulders and the nape of the neck. That is the most important part. This is how the garment is draped."[4] From then on, the rest of the model comes naturally.

Yves Saint Laurent very soon understood that fashion cannot content itself merely with embellishing women. Women also need to be reassured, given confidence, be enabled to take on the new role that they are now assuming in a society permeated with the ideas of feminism. The "liberated" woman of the late twentieth century demands an elegance of a new type. She no longer lives in the shadow of her male companion, devoted to the duties of wife and mother. She has taken her own destiny in hand and has built an identity outside the family home. She has to convince others of her legitimacy in this new use of the first-person singular. In 1966, Saint Laurent first asserted: "Elegance has been transformed. Attraction has taken its place. Affectation, starchiness, and the too-perfect have begun to irritate us. A well-dressed woman today is one who knows how to construct a certain harmony between her clothes and her personality."

The allure of the Saint Laurent woman is indefinably in her diversity, enabling her to express the complex facets of her personality. She is a woman living in a world whose frontiers have expanded, whose curiosity is unbridled, from New York to Katmandu, from Goa to Marrakech. She rejects middle-class conventions and is tempted by forbidden games; she takes the risk of veering off the signposted path. She seeks to blur the trail in a piquant exercise in seduction and is never where you expect her to be. Behind her calm exterior, she hides a passionate nature, in the image of Catherine Deneuve in *Belle de jour.*

The sexual liberation that occurred in the late 1960s was followed by a true relaxation of morals and appearances. The girls who attended Woodstock were too quick to reject elegance. The word sounded to them like a mistake, a ridiculous anachronism. The hippie ideal did a great deal of harm to the luxury trades. But Yves Saint Laurent revived their fortunes with a sensational collection in the summer of 1971. He brought back the need for sophistication in style, and flowing, draped dresses, and high heels. Katmandu was just a mirage, the gurus merely businessmen in disguise. The glamour and the impudent femininity were built on the invention of "retro" fashion. The rest of the fashion world soon followed, taking the road to the flea market and relearning from the 1930s the secrets of how to look chic, the allure of the divine women, Greta Garbo and Marlene Dietrich.

By designing the immediate future of fashion, the couturier demonstrated his intuition about the period, the emerging sensitivity to a moment that will become tomorrow's truth. Despite his distant expression of a dreamer, he could see where things were heading. Marguerite Duras understood him: "I want to say that what he does is what one did not know one was expecting."[5] Yves Saint Laurent invented the foundations of the modern wardrobe, which remains the foundations of modern fashion. With his first three-piece pantsuit translated into feminine terms, he offered a basis for the wardrobe of a woman of action, reproducing all the advantages of a male business suit: the comfort and security of a well-made garment, the modern armor with which to face the world with confidence. It was not a matter of aping masculine tastes or of copying or emasculating them. There was no suffragette spirit behind this borrowing from male fashion. Even taking inspiration from gangsters such as Al Capone, using pinstripes and wide lapels, the suit became feminine when matched with silk muslin blouses and cummerbunds. In 1975, in the famous photograph published in *Vogue*, Helmut Newton immortalized the power of attraction that this genre exercised at the limits of androgyny. In a street lit by the lampposts of a film noir, a woman with hair plastered flat in the Spanish style poses gallantly, cigarette in hand, in her tight-fitting, padded-shouldered jacket. But the pants legs that widen into a skirt and the blouse with its collar tied in a floppy bow contribute every ambiguity to the scene. She is not a tomboy, but a worthy daughter of Chanel who, in the 1920–1930 decade, remained feminine in her bell-bottoms or in a British tweed jacket. "La grande mademoiselle" is one of the masters who, along with Monsieur Dior, taught Saint Laurent, by his own admission, the rituals of haute couture.

In 1966, the tuxedo transposed into the feminine caused a sensation when it erupted into receptions, worn by young women who were delighted to be able to reject the outmoded full-length dress. Extracting a garment from its original context revitalized couture, through the shock of its being used in exactly the opposite way. With the decontextualization of the male wardrobe, Yves Saint Laurent explored the qualities of the male business suit and sportswear. In 1962, the Norman shirt inaugurated a genealogy of models of functional origin. The way in which their shape was so suited to their intended purpose makes them important, even bestowing a nobility, due to the way they have withstood the test of time. The sporting spirit stimulates urban elegance and pushes aside the tradition of the tailored suit. The sailor's peacoat, the sweater, the officer's greatcoat, and the trench coat write a new chapter in the book begun by Chanel in the 1910–1920 decade, that of a timeless look. They perfectly illustrate the couturier's aphorism: "My dream is to give women the basis for a classic wardrobe, which, escaping the fashion of the moment, will give them greater confidence in themselves." With this revolution of the new masculine-feminine gender, the couturier dressed his female contemporaries in everyday garments, those that can illustrate his famous maker's mark, as well as clothing seen in the street. "The women of Saint Laurent have come out of the harem, the château and even the suburbs, they can be seen in the streets, the metros, the Prisunic, the Stock Exchange," stated Marguerite Duras.[6] When they want to come close to fulfilling their dream of haute couture, the Saint Laurent Rive Gauche boutiques meet their expectations by offering them an affordable style. Those that feel they will look overdressed in haute couture garments adopt this new brand with enthusiasm. Launched at his boutique on the rue de Tournon, Saint Laurent Rive Gauche experienced the first spectacular success of couturier ready-to-wear. "The street and me, it's a love story," claimed Saint Laurent in 1971, five years after his pioneering initiative.

Elegance, according to the couturier, is a happy woman with a man at her side. A sweater and a black skirt with a large costume jewelry pin is enough to make her desirable. But a woman who uses the ambiguous charm of androgyny adds to her palette of attractions the strangeness of the metamorphosis of a Dr. Jekyll into a Miss Hyde. The woman protected from outside pressure by her daywear is transformed into a terrifying goddess sublimated by an "almost shameless dress in the evening. Extremely elegant, but enormously revealing." She is ready to play any role, any drama, all the repertoire of the heroines created by the pen of Shakespeare or Proust, painted by Renoir or Velásquez. The couturier also sees her as the Cubist reconstruction of a multiple reality, a paper cut-out by Matisse, a wild vision by Cocteau. But, unlike these favorite authors or painters, he works with a mobile material, a fabric: "You can produce a pretty drawing, you can put all the skill of your profession into the drawing, but if you do not have the right material, you will lose your dress. What causes anguish is not to be unable to decide where to put the pockets or the belt, the shape of the neck or the volume, the anguish is when you have to deal with the fabric and the color, when you have to become deeply involved with the material in the same way as the painter with his paintbrush and the sculptor with his clay. And it is the material that has to submit if a dress is to match the way you imagined it." The most difficult thing for Saint Laurent was to capture the colors that haunted his imagination since his childhood in Oran and his discovery of Morocco. Paris is a gray city, devoid of color. So the couturier embarked on his voyages around his drawing table. He translated his admiration for art and literature into a dress. He brought back from mental excursions to Russia, Spain, and India visions of women decked out in traditional costumes that have swapped modernity with folklore. Great washes of color worked like a painter in a series of breaks, removed any traditionalism from Slavic blouses and petticoats, gypsy silk skirts and transparent blouses, until they were ready to be seen in Saint-Germain-des-Prés or

Saint-Tropez. The girls with sparkling eyes under their turbans illuminated the penumbra through Guy Bourdin's lens. The 1970s are ending and the sophistication launched by the couturier is adopted by the younger generation of future "female combatants." In checks and wide shoulder pads, they asserted their desire to become career women. In Yves Saint Laurent jacket, skirt, boots, and cape they set out to win power in the business world. In the early 1980s, the creator designed a trompe l'oeil style that adorned their figures with shorter dresses, deeper necklines, wider shoulders.

In the late twentieth century, having constructed modernity in style, Yves Saint Laurent embarked on a quest for the ideal of an unchangeable wardrobe consisting of smart suits and beautiful skirts. "Today, it is extreme simplicity that gives me my greatest joy. Getting to it being everything and nothing at the same time," he confided in Laurence Benaïm.[7] After the retrospective fashion parade of 2002, the couturier only thought of "the modern woman who has no encumbrances. . . . Men hate women in fancy costume. To get noticed, you don't need a red pompon and an aigrette. What matters is technique. Otherwise, you are just gathering a mass of fabric, pinning on flowers and a green bird of paradise." On the one hand, there should be flowing movement, the flutter of muslin dresses that hint at a body in the transparency of a color. And then tailored pantsuits, tuxedos, boleros, with strong lines but narrowed reveres, pants with wide, loose legs. He was no longer interested in changing fashion each season and in fact, this had never guided his creativity; but he was tempted to create prototypes that will never go out of fashion, which, like jeans, are the perfect garment. Questioned in 1994 on what was the most important point for him, Yves Saint Laurent replied: "It's style. I do not change, I become deeper. The cut changes. Fashion passes, style remains."[8]

Florence Müller

1. *Elle,* France, January 27, 1992.
2. *Yves Saint Laurent et la photographie de mode,* Paris, Albin, Michel, 1977.
3. Exhibition catalogue "Fashion—1968–1990," Sezon Museum of Art, November 14–December 26, 1990.
4. *Elle,* France, December 25, 1995.
5. Exhibition catalogue "Fashion—1968–1990," Sezon Museum of Art, November 14–December 26, 1990.
6. *Ibid.*
7. Laurence Benaïm, *Yves Saint Laurent,* Paris, Éditions Grasset & Fasquelle, 1993.
8. *Glamour,* France, May 1, 1994.

AT THE PENCIL POINT

The starting point of each Yves Saint Laurent collection is marked by the arrival of the drawings in the studio. At that moment, the creative act materializes into the most free, most natural, and yet the most surprising spontaneity of the couturier, who sketches the images of the dresses as they form in his imagination, without any preconceptions or planning. These drawings are abundant and come easily, after which they are subjected to rigorous selection. When he began, Yves Saint Laurent would produce up to one thousand drawings, but only retain around two hundred. It is a moment of jubilation when anything is possible, when the dream has not yet been destroyed by the logic of the textiles to be used. But what makes Yves Saint Laurent's sketches of such amazing quality are their closeness to their final destination. The sketches that are chosen possess all of the indications that the workshops need for cutting and mounting the working drawing into a fabric pattern, thus avoiding the need to extrapolate or compromise the initial intention, which would distort the inspiration in its pure state.

STYLE IN MOVEMENT

"ALL MY DRESSES ORIGINATE WITH A GESTURE. A DRESS THAT DOES NOT REFLECT OR DOES NOT MAKE ONE THINK OF A GESTURE IS NOT RIGHT. ONCE THE GESTURE IN QUESTION HAS BEEN FOUND, THEN ONE CAN CHOOSE THE COLOR, THE FINAL SHAPE, THE FABRICS, BUT NOT BEFORE. IN REALITY, ONE NEVER STOPS LEARNING IN THIS PROFESSION."

Yves Saint Laurent, quoted by Laurence Benaïm, in *Yves Saint Laurent* (Paris: Grasset, 1993), p. 305.

Like a preliminary sketch produced by a painter, Yves Saint Laurent's drawings define all of the important points that define the model. The general outline constructs the silhouette and the articulation between the human body and the garment. But it says even more than that. The sketch suggests the garment in movement on a moving body. It foresees the position and anticipates its gestures. The summer dress created in 1958, when Saint Laurent was with Dior, has remained famous as the prototype of the *Trapeze* line. Yet even then, the young couturier was seeking to extract from this logic the line for the season, as launched by his mentor Christian Dior, to become the predominant style, that of a bust released from all constraints through being unleashed by the "Trapeze." His sketches marvelously predict how this would be expressed on the body: a leg escaping from a wide slit, the curve of a bare back in the austerity of a sheath, the twirling hemline of a fitted coat or an immaculate dress, the heaving of a bust in the "Tulip" dress of 1962 or 1964.

1

32

35

Robe lamage noir
s/Ama

LEFUR 5673 col noir-

Chapeau - Grande forme avec noeud

1 Collier Superbe 6 Rgs multicolors

Bo. Assortis _

42

13

62   Robe Habillée
s/ Muriel
Shantung naturel
PETILLAULT
6111 naturel

base en shantung noir
B-D-M 4051 noir

rose en Murel 6147 noir

5B Desmes 5612 Bis/30 Naturel

Capeline paille d'Italie et velours noir-

B.O jules s/Jais   gants noirs

. Hamon.
Ceinture vernis
noir

Anseline
5 B/5 2164/22
Jean

36

chapeau :
petit pour turban
de velours vert
avec Noeud de
velours Noir sur
le dessous -
voilette de tulle
Noir point
d'esprit
Nouée derrière
le chapeau -

M ✗ 1066
S. Pierre

S/ Mounia

Robe en Grain de
Poudre Noir.
Moreau 981710
col et poignets
velours noir
Moreau 1000/NR

gants chevreau rose/fushia.

1 collier, ras le cou -
Brodie épis en demi-cercle
avec palme pendante de
pierres irisées turquoiseetmauve-
sur ruban de velours Noir.

Escarpins
crêpe Noir
drapés -

de chaque côté de la tête
2 branches GOOSSENS (B.D)
Guirlande de
fleurs et Noeud
métal OR et
au milieu 1
fleur GOOSSENS
métal OR
(B.D)

Musée

134 4347 p

Jacqueline / Sadija

Robe de gazar blanc
Abraham 8003/100

interieur en taffetas
Blanc — Broche 103

1 epaule brodée GOOSSENS
sur la robe Noeud
cocarde de métal OR —

escarpins gazar blanc
assorti à la robe
talons en satin Blc
VII 93

Nomad
3445 846 631
NB

musée

53

6939

Claudia/ Jean Pierre.

Veste smoking de grain de
pauche noir et satin revers.
Gandini 2672 col 3
Buche 210 coe NR

6939bis J. Pierre.

Pantalon idem.

- ras de cou de
strass diamants
G. 36

AH 51-97

Sandals
plate forme
Satin noir

Fil de 7/6
Fil de 7/6

45
Musée

7145,

Katoucha/Arlette

Robe drapée
de satin noir
Clerici 2396
the NR 09
Irmula 2228
col 0009

- Bo pendantes
grande fleurs de
saphir fleurs roses
- et chute de perles
irisée verte, roses
et pierres fleurs
et verres B. 4

sandals
de satin
noir
à brids
Chevilles

FM le 16/06

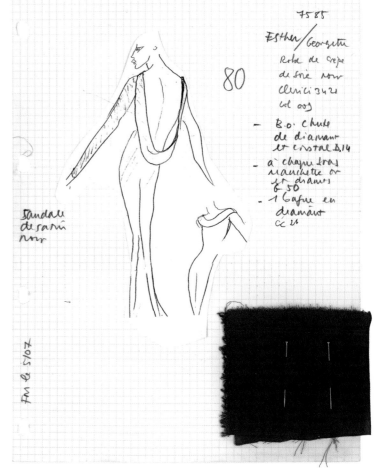

7585

Esther/Georgette

Robe de crêpe
de soie noir
Clerici 3421
col 009

- B.o. chute
de diamant
et cristal B.14

- à chaque bras
manchette or
et diamant
G.50

- 1 bague en
diamant
CC 21

80

sandale
de satin
noir

FM le 5/07

7   8

"ELEGANCE IS BEING NOTICED WHILE WEARING A BLACK DRESS. IT'S BEING AT EASE. IT'S THE ATTITUDE. IT IS NOT WRINKLES OR WHITE HAIR THAT AGE A WOMAN, IT IS HER GESTURES. THAT IS WHERE MY ACCESSORIES PLAY AN IMPORTANT ROLE. A SCARF THAT ONE CAN PLAY WITH, A PURSE ON A LONG STRAP WORN BANDOLIER-FASHION SO THAT THE HANDS ARE FREE—THERE IS NOTHING UGLIER THAN A PURSE THAT DANGLES AT THE END OF AN ARM. A FLEXIBLE BELT—ALWAYS A CHAIN—THAT NICELY EMPHASIZES THE HIPS, AND POCKETS. MY ACCESSORIES ARE GESTURES."

Yves Saint Laurent, quoted by Laurence Benaïm, in *Yves Saint Laurent,* op. cit., p. 171.

THE BODY REVEALED

"THE NAKED BODY OF A WOMAN, WHOM I HAVE TO DRESS WITHOUT CURBING THE FREEDOM OF HER NATURAL MOVEMENTS. IN SHORT, MY PROFESSION IS THE LOVING DIALOGUE OF THIS NAKED WOMAN WITH ALL THE MAGIC SPELLS OF THE WRAPPING OF MY FABRICS."

Yves Saint Laurent, quoted by Laurence Benaïm, in *Yves Saint Laurent,* op. cit., p. 399.

The outline of a clever cut or the audacious treatment of drapery exposes the beauty of the female body more certainly than mere nudity. Dresses mutate into swimwear, a half-dress is kept in place by a few pink bows at the waist and hips, décolletés dare to drop dizzily to the waste. These games of revealing and hiding exhibit the power of female sensuality. The female back in the shape of a lyre, in 1970, appears through a window of lace mesh; Zizi's legs in the sequined sweater-dress, breasts offered in their black velvet setting.

René
avec (3119) | Blanche
cape de   Muriel
laine-mèche   3044.
blanche
Mme Closet

138

Blanche

54

crêpe noir
ABRAHAM
5300 col 60

Clip perle crochée
dans jais.

ch. satin noir

9

Zibeline   1656

117 Elsa
     Catherine

Gandini 589.

Brivet 413 201.

- tulan velours bleu -
  sandale daim noir -

10

1205 X

Catherine / Edua
Robe fourreau dos nu
Jersey de soie noir
RACINE Byzance

paletot de plumes
blanches autruches
et plumes argentées
Mr Lemarié

Collier ras de cou gros pavés rectan.
-gulaires diamant Ceillel -
BO - carés stars diamant
Sabbagh -
2 bracelets (anciens) Goossens
argent et diamant

12,9
Nuria

FM 29-12 82

11

115
M

2055°X
Catherine/Kiat
Robe longue en crêpe
marocain rouge
Branchiui 23508/265

B.O BOUTRON
Carré métal
gris + strass
avec cube
cristal et Boule
corail strass NOIRS

2 bracelets cubes
diamants avec
chute Boule de
corail · BOUTRON

Sandale
crêpe Rouge
avec bride.

KM 4/1

12

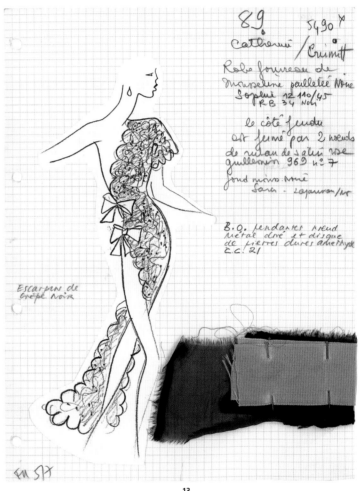

89
Catherine/Cruinitt

5490°

Robe fourreau de
Mousseline pailletée Noire
Sophie 12 110/45
RB 34 Noir

le côté fendu
est fermé par 2 nœuds
de ruban de satin rose
guillermin 969 n° 7
fond mousseline
sara - Lajauron/12

B.O. pendantes nœud
métal doré et disque
de pierres dures améthyste
2.c./21

Escarpin de
crêpe noir

KM 57

13

14_1

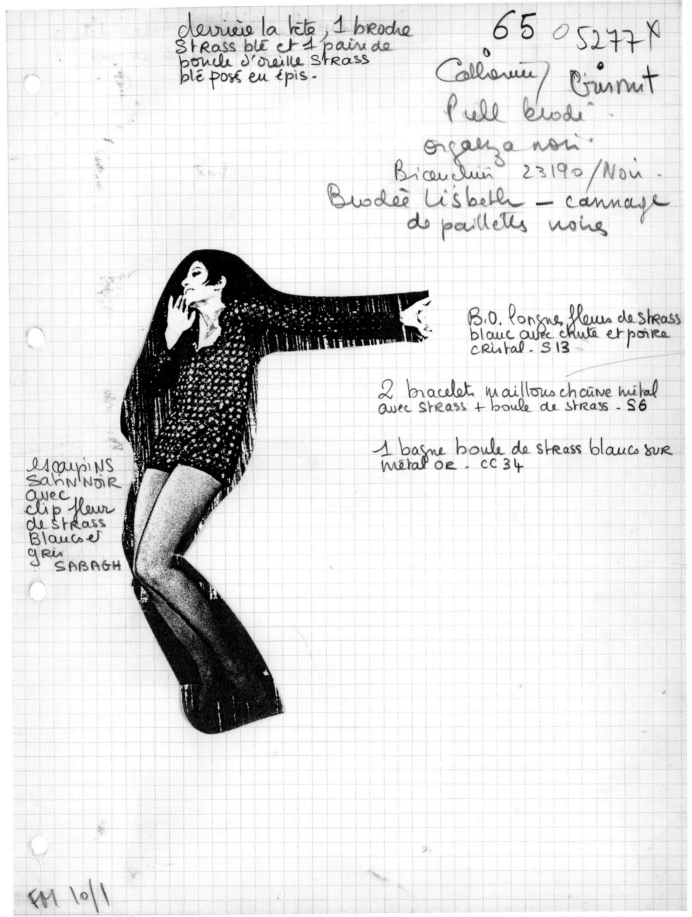

derrière la tête, 1 broche
Strass blé et 1 paire de
boucle d'oreille strass
blé posé en épis.

65 05277 X
Collhonin Grimnit
Pull brodé.
organza noir.
Biancluin 23190/Noir.
Brodèe Lisbeth — cannage
de paillettes noirs

B.O. longue fleurs de strass
blanc avec chute et poire
cristal. S13

2 bracelets maillons chaîne métal
avec strass + boule de strass - S6

1 bague boule de strass blancs sur
métal or. CC 34

Escarpins
satin noir
avec
clip fleur
de strass
Blancs et
gris
SABAGH

FM 10/1

REDEFINING THE SILHOUETTE

"MY ESSENTIAL RULE IS TO ELONGATE WOMEN, AND ABOVE ALL, TO MAKE THEM LOOK THINNER. AFTER THAT, ALL THAT REMAINS IS TO MAKE THEIR JEWELRY LOOK BIGGER. AND THEY ARE DELIGHTED!"

Yves Saint Laurent, quoted by Laurence Benaïm, in *Yves Saint Laurent,* op. cit., p. 173.

The garment, in its unique volumes, magnifies and amplifies the natural body, eventually making its mark on the original contours. It then seems to liberate itself from the laws of gravity and anatomy. Skirts swell into bubbles, balls, clouds, banners. . . . But for a surprising bride of 1965, her baggy, large-knitted dress protected her body in an impermeable cocoon of wool.

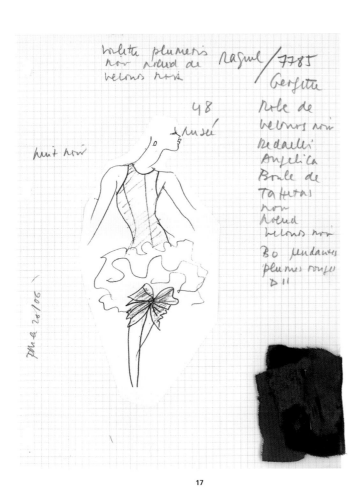

Violette plumeris
noir noeud de
velours noir

Raquel / 7785

Georgette

48

Huit noir

Nusé

Robe de
velours noir
Medailli
Angelica
Boule de
Tahitas
noir
noeud
velours noir

Bo pendants
plumes rouge
D 11

PMR 20/06

17

2122
Atelier Mme Felisa
S/ mercedes

Cape de velours noir
avec capuche de
renard blanc
LEONARD 11862
col noir

83

3

18

99   2155 X

Mme Felisa
S/ Kerat

Robe de taffetas gris
Bianchini 21212
col libellule

B.O fleurs strass
centre jais et gouttes
jais

2 Bracelets fines fleurs strass
Bague ronde strass bleu-pâle
et perle

satin noir et strass

19

60   5611 Y

Musée Jacqueline / Katoucha

Robe courte en
organza - satin jaçonné
Noir
Taroni 9516/Nr

Bo pendantes pierre verte et metal
(G.527)   or travaille et
feuille or

Bouton
Dessus
fronces
jais

Sandales
SAHININ
Bas chairs

20

49

3147 Esther 192

mariée
68

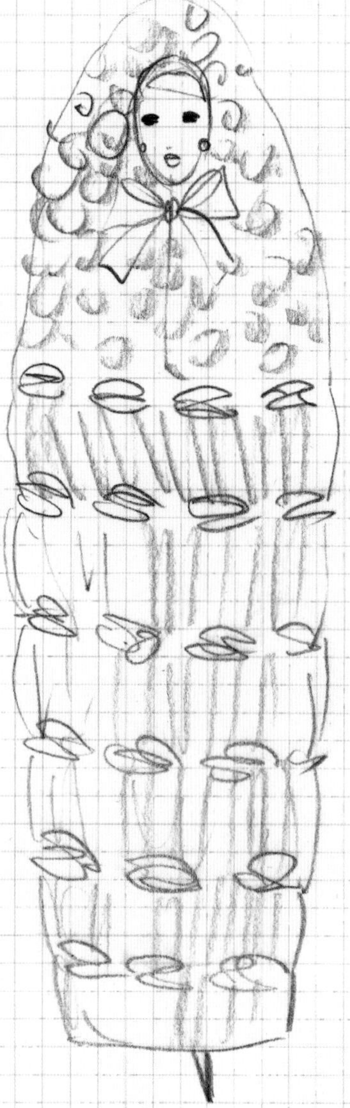

fond taffetas
blanc

10g

1

"Trapeze" Dress
Yves Saint Laurent for Christian Dior
Spring–Summer 1958

Coarse woolen fabric by Rodier. Straw and velvet hat. Leather gloves and pumps.

Metropolitan Museum of Art, New York, 1983. Palace of Fine Arts, Beijing, 1985. Musée des Arts de la Mode, Paris, 1986. Tretyakov Gallery, Moscow, 1986. State Hermitage Museum, St. Petersburg, 1987. Art Gallery, Sydney, 1987. Sezon Museum of Art, Tokyo, 1990.

Publication

Paris Match, France, March 1, 1958.

2

Formal Dress
Fall–Winter 1962

Worsted by Lesur. Knotted velvet hat. Metal and bead costume drop earrings. Colored bead necklace and bracelet. Suede gloves and pumps.

Metropolitan Museum of Art, New York, 1983. Palace of Fine Arts, Beijing, 1985. Musée des Arts de la Mode, Paris, 1986. Tretyakov Gallery, Moscow, 1986. State Hermitage Museum, St. Petersburg, 1987. Art Gallery, Sydney, 1987.

Publication

The New York Times (drawing), United States, August 12, 1962.

3

Cocktail Dress
Spring–Summer 1964

Pétillault shantung by Brossin de Méré. Rose in Hurel silk. Shantung and velvet hat. Colored bead drop earrings. Leather gloves and pumps.
Made to order for HRH Princess Grace of Monaco.

Musée des Arts de la Mode, Paris, 1986. Art Gallery, Sydney, 1987.

Publications

Elle, France, February 28, 1964.
Vogue, France, April 1964.
Vogue, United States, March 1964.
Harper's Bazaar, United States, March 1964.

4

Cocktail Dress
Fall–Winter 1982

Barathea by Dormeuil. Velvet by Moreau. Patent leather belt by Hamon. Velvet hat. Short tulle veil. Stone pendant earrings. Rhinestone and metal pin. Kid gloves. Crêpe pumps.

5

Wedding Gown
Fall–Winter 1988

Silk gazar by Abraham. Metal and rock crystal earrings and pin by Goossens. Silk gazar pumps.

Publication

Vogue, United States, November 1988.

6

Tuxedo
Fall–Winter 1996

Barathea and satin by Gandini. Rhinestone and metal choker necklace. Satin sandals.

Fondation Pierre Bergé–Yves Saint Laurent, Paris, 2005.

Publication

Vogue, Italy, September 1996.

7

Evening Gown
Fall–Winter 1997

Draped silk satin by Clerici. Stone and rhinestone pendant earrings by Boutron. Satin sandals.

8

Evening Gown
Fall–Winter 1999

Silk crêpe by Clerici. Rhinestone and metal pendant earrings, cuffs, and ring. Satin sandals.

Publication

Vogue, Italy, September 1997.

9

Evening Gown
Fall–Winter 1965

Silk crêpe by Abraham. Faceted cabochon, jet, and metal stud earrings. Suede pumps.

Publication

Vogue, United States, September 1965.

10

Evening Gown
Fall–Winter 1970

Woolen crêpe by Gandini. Lace back by Brivet. Velvet turban. Metal and rhinestone stud earrings. Suede gloves. Platform sandals in patent leather and suede.

Metropolitan Museum of Art, New York, 1983. Palace of Fine Arts, Beijing, 1985. Musée des Arts de la Mode, Paris, 1986. Art Gallery, Sydney, 1987. Musée de la Mode, Marseille, 1993.

Publications

Vogue, France, September 1970.
Harper's Bazaar, United States, January 1979.

11

Evening Gown
Spring–Summer 1983

Sheath dress in silk jersey by Racine. Faceted cabochon and metal necklace by Caillol. Metal and rhinestone cuffs by Goossens. Rhinestone earrings. Silk crêpe and rhinestone pumps.

Publication

L'Officiel, France, March 1983.

12

Evening Gown
Spring–Summer 1985

Silk crêpe by Gandini. Rhinestone, metal, and glass bead pendant earrings and bracelets. Silk crêpe strappy sandals.
Made to order for Nan Kempner.

Palace of Fine Arts, Beijing, 1985. Musée des Arts de la Mode, Paris, 1986. Tretyakov Gallery, Moscow, 1986. State Hermitage Museum, St. Petersburg, 1987. Art Gallery, Sydney, 1987.

Publication

L'Officiel, France, March 1985.

13

Evening Gown
Fall–Winter 1990

Embroidered lace by Sophie and silk satin ribbons by Guillemin. Amethyst and metal pendant earrings. Silk crêpe pumps.

Musée de la Mode, Marseille, 1993.

Publications

Harper's Bazaar, France, September 1990.
L'Officiel, France, September 1990.

14_1, 14_2

Evening Tunic in Tribute to Zizi Jeanmaire
Spring–Summer 1990

Embroidered with sequins and bugle beads by Lisbeth. Rhinestone and metal pendant earrings and bracelets by Sabbagh. Silk satin pumps.
Made to order for Princess Diane von Fürstenberg.

Fondation Pierre Bergé–Yves Saint Laurent, Paris, 2007.

Publications

Harper's Bazaar, France, March 1990.
Vogue, United States, April 1990.
L'Officiel, France, May 1990.

15

Evening Gown
Fall–Winter 1993

Moreau velvet. Embroidered lace by Marescot. Silk satin bow by Abraham. Rhinestone, bead, and metal pendant earrings. Silk satin bar shoes.

Musée de la Mode, Marseille, 1993.

16

Evening Gown
Fall–Winter 1993

Velvet by Moreau. Silk faille by Taroni. Tulle bustier by Rodolphe Simon. Rhinestone and metal pendant earrings by Sabbagh. Silk satin bar shoes.

Musée de la Mode, Marseille, 1993.

Publications

Vogue, France, September 1993.
Interview, United States, October 1993.

17

Evening Gown
Fall–Winter 2000, no. 48

Velvet by Hurel. Silk taffeta shirring by Buche. Violet velvet bow. Stone, feather, and metal pendant earrings. Silk satin bar shoes.

18

Evening Ensemble
Fall–Winter 1977

Velvet cape by Léonard. Fox-fur hood by Garande. Chain-knit sweater. Velvet pants by Léonard. Velvet and passementerie cap. Sunglasses. Leather and mink gloves and boots.

Metropolitan Museum of Art, New York, 1983. Palace of Fine Arts, Beijing, 1985. Musée des Arts de la Mode, Paris, 1986.

Publication

L'Officiel, United States, October 1, 1977.

19

Evening Gown
Fall–Winter 1981, no. 99

Taffeta by Bianchini. Rhinestone, metal, and bead pendant earrings. Rhinestone and metal bracelets. Silk satin and rhinestone pumps.

Metropolitan Museum of Art, New York, 1983. Musée des Arts de la Mode, Paris, 1986. Sezon Museum of Art, Tokyo, 1990.

20

Evening Gown
Spring–Summer 1991, no. 60

Patterned organza by Taroni. Metal and bead pendant earrings. Silk satin sandals.
Made to order for Mrs. Oscar de La Renta.

21

Bridal Gown
Fall–Winter 1965

Hand-knitted woolen tricot by Closset. Silk satin ribbons. Leather gloves. Silk satin pumps with buckles.

Musée des Arts de la Mode, Paris, 1986. Tretyakov Gallery, Moscow, 1986. State Hermitage Museum, St. Petersburg, 1987. Art Gallery, Sydney, 1987.

Publications

WWD (drawing), United States, August 3, 1965.
Paris Jour, France, August 30, 1965.
France-Soir, France, August 29, 1965.
Elle, France, September 2, 1985.

THE YVES SAINT LAURENT REVOLUTION

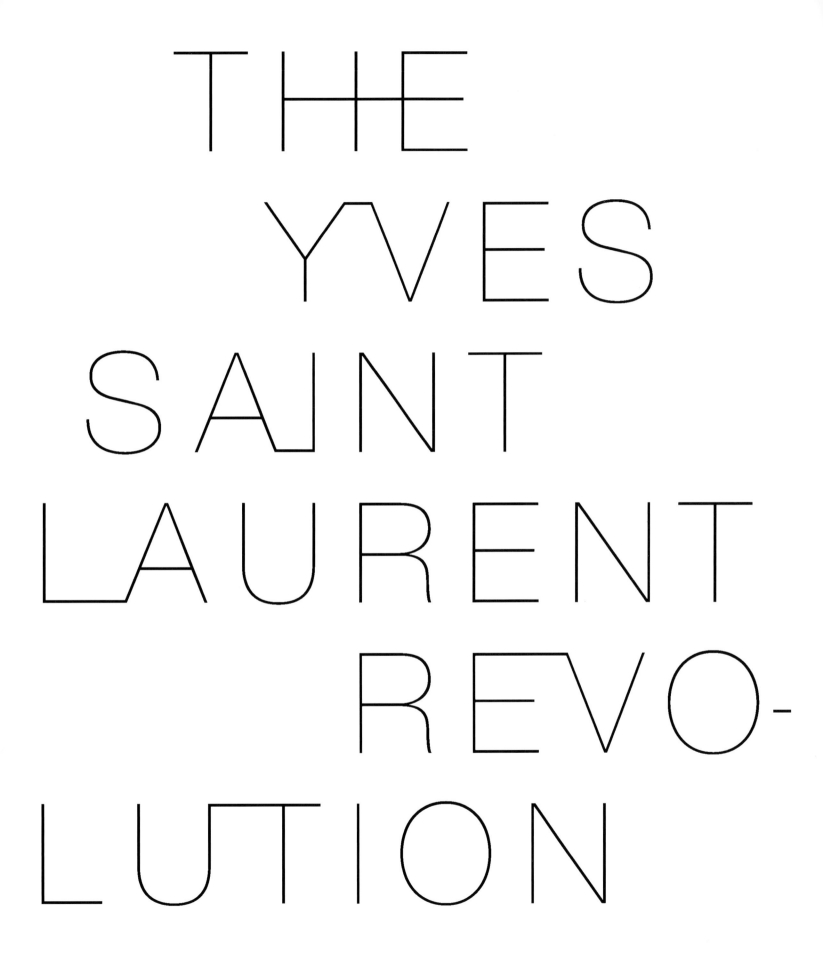

With the tuxedo jacket and pants, Yves Saint Laurent dressed women in the symbols of male power. These suits inspired by male clothing signified a revolution in the history of dress, in that women could now wear pants, day or night. The vision of the androgynous woman with a slim, elongated silhouette, like that of a teenager, is still current, and pants remain an essential item in the modern female wardrobe. Sportswear and uniforms have also been reinterpreted in female versions. But dresses and skirts have not been consigned to the dungeon of history. They are revisited in terms of the modality of the female condition and of a femininity consisting of multiple facets. The diversions of lingerie enrich haute couture with a theme that was unknown hitherto. All of these new principles offer a register of infinite interpretations, which regularly will bring them back to the avenue Marceau collections.

MASCULINE-FEMININE

"A WOMAN IS ONLY ATTRACTIVE IN PANTS IF SHE WEARS THEM WITH ALL HER FEMININITY. NOT LIKE A GEORGE SAND. PANTS ARE COQUETTISH, AN ADDITIONAL CHARM, NOT A SIGN OF EQUALITY OR ENFRANCHISEMENT. LIBERTY AND EQUALITY ARE NOT ACHIEVED BY WEARING BREECHES — THEY ARE A STATE OF MIND."

Yves Saint Laurent, quoted by Laurence Benaïm, in *Yves Saint Laurent*, op. cit., p. 157.

The cross-dressing suits of 1967 or Broadway-inspired fashions of 1978 give a liberated air to women who are "unsubjugated." The safari jacket borrowed from the Afrika Korps in 1968, the 1967 trench-coat, the 1971 blazer, the 1967 officer's jacket, and the aviator's blouson are all variations on uniform that make one look twice. With his peacoats, duffle coats, and Norman peasant blouses of 1962, then the tunics, chasubles, and peasant skirts, Yves Saint Laurent incorporated the essential qualities of the work garment, namely functionality and timelessness. Overalls, dungarees, the jumpsuit, shorts, the rollneck sweater, are all offered as alternatives to the tailored suit.

22

7003

24

25

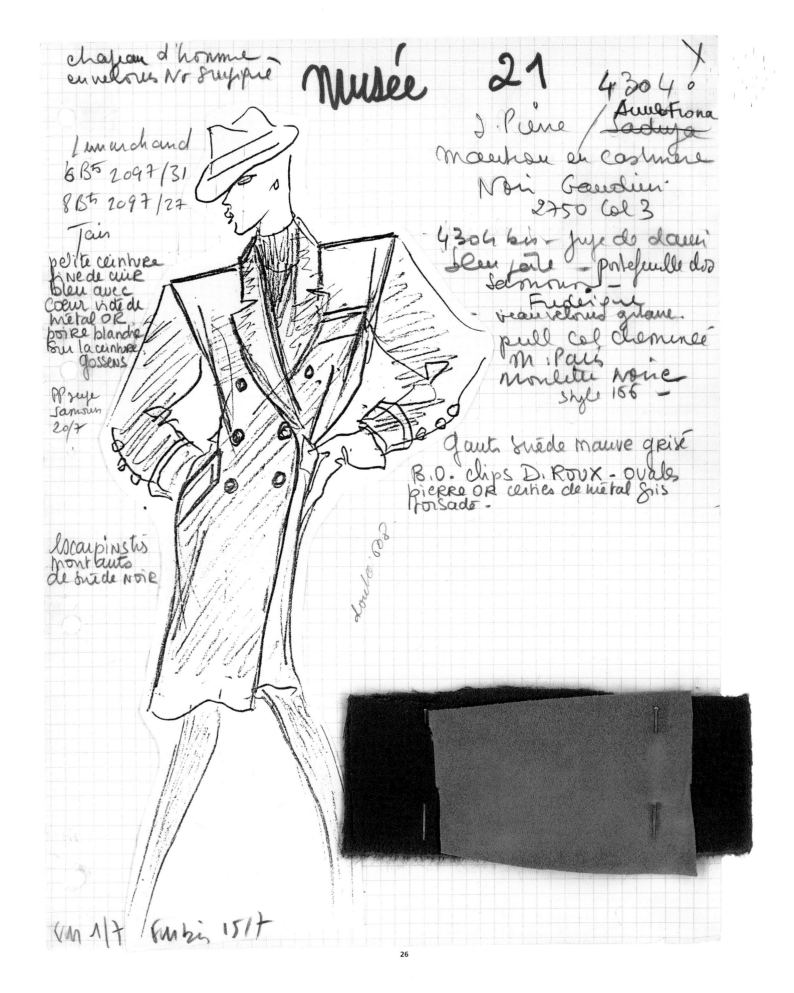

chapeau d'homme
en velours Nr 8 supprimé

Musée 21 43040

L.marchand
6 Bts 2097/31
8 Bts 2097/27

Tan

petite ceinture
fine de cuir
bleu avec
coeur vide de
métal OR
poire blanche
sur la ceinture
gossens

PP.suye
Samson
20/7

lscarpins.ts
montants
de suède NOIR

J. Piene / AnneFiona ~~Saduja~~
manteau en cashmere
Noir Gaudier
2750 Col 3

43040 bis - jupe de drap
bleu pâle - portefeuille dos
Salmson -
Fuselique
veau velours gitane.
pull col cheminée
M. Paris
moulette noire
style 166 -

gants suède mauve grisé
B.O. clips D. ROUX - ovales
pierre OR certies de métal gris
torsadé.

loulou 608.

VM 1/7   Embis 15/7

26

59

Robe d'après midi
Tunique de jersey
de soie noire

1962
Pea jacket
gold buttons

white shantung
pants

Navy leather
sandal

29

30

blanc

rose blanc

1,80

1,20

blanc

Catherine
4119

Esther
Danielle!
2007

veste +
robe

2068
Nicole

31   32

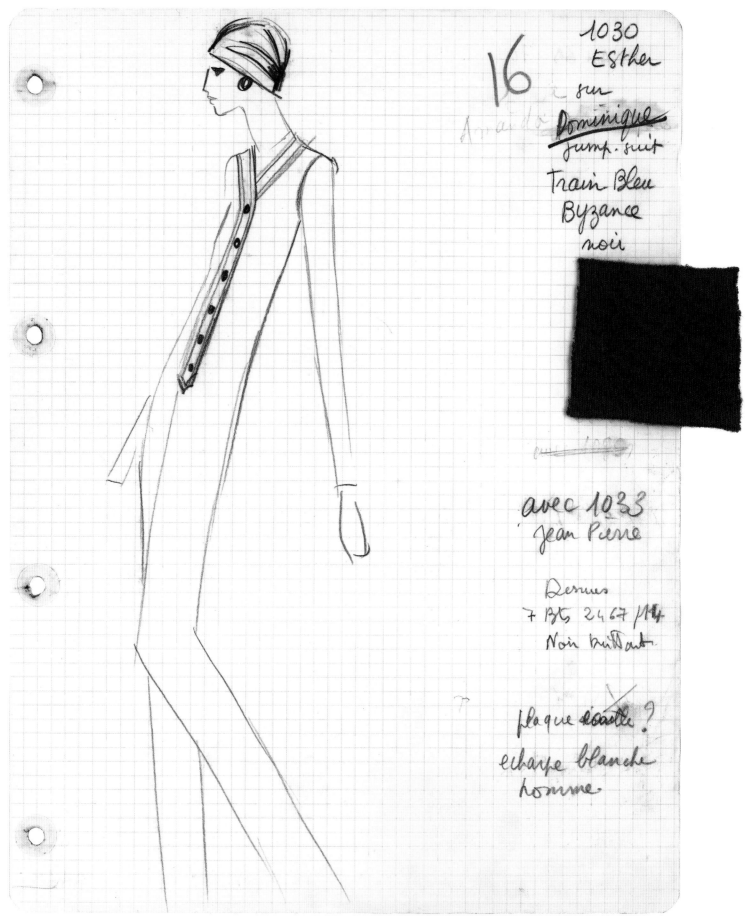

35

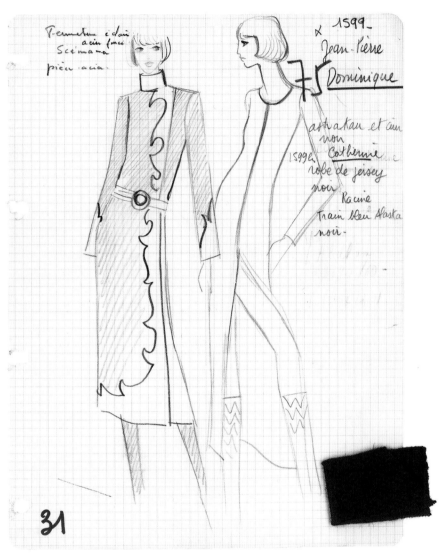

31

R. J. Pierre.
4 BS 318/2e
6 à " /15

2106
Jean Pierre

68 Jacqueline

short gabardine
blanc
PERCEVAL-SEKERS
4748 / blanc
Blazer gabardine
marine
DORMEUIL
981.778

Catherine 2106 bis
blouse bain de soleil
Parthenon marine

J

Bob blanc
Rayinde bleu verni
noir
1 carré de mousseline
écossaise Canard /jaune
noué deux fois autour
du cou
5213 /11

4

7762

Gergette

Amalia

Sweater

40

22
Pantsuit
Spring–Summer 1967
Jacket and pants in striped wool gabardine by Raimon. Cotton shirt. Silk tie. Buttoned cuffs. Patent leather sandals.
Publications
Harper's Bazaar, United States, March 1967.
Life, United States, March 3, 1967.
L'Officiel, France, March 1967.
Vogue, France, March 1967.

23
Skirtsuit
Spring–Summer 1967
Jacket, vest, and skirt in striped flannel by Dormeuil. Cotton shirt. Felt and grosgrain hat. Buttoned cuffs. Leather pumps with buckles.
Publications
Elle, France, March 2, 1967.
Vogue, France, March 1967.
L'Officiel, France, March 1967.
WWD, United States, October 1967.

24
Skirtsuit
Fall–Winter 1975
Tweed de chine by Besson. Blouse with floppy bow cravat in crêpe de chine by Abraham. Knitted cap. Metal cuff buttons. Lizard-skin sandals.

25
Pantsuit
Spring–Summer 1978
Chevron-patterned woolen fabric by Besson. Blouse with floppy bow cravat and crêpe de chine belt by Abraham. Straw boater with taffeta ribbon. Metal "snail" stud earrings. Leather sandals.
Made to order for Mrs. Oscar Wyatt.
Metropolitan Museum of Art, New York, 1983. Palace of Fine Arts, Beijing, 1985. State Hermitage Museum, St. Petersburg, 1987. Art Gallery, Sydney, 1987. Sezon Museum of Art, Tokyo, 1990.
Publications
Vogue, France, March 1978.
L'Officiel, France, April 1978.

26
Daytime Ensemble
Fall–Winter 1988
Cashmere coat by Gandini. Suede wraparound skirt. Woolen sweater by Michel Paris. Velvet and trimming hat. Metal cabochon earrings. Gloves. Suede walking shoes.
Made to order for Catherine Deneuve.

27
Pantsuit
Fall–Winter 1999
Tweed Holland & Sherry woolen sweater. Wooden stud earrings. Suede and leather gloves. Suede pumps.
Publication
Hola, Spain, January 1999.

28
Daytime Ensemble
Spring–Summer 1962
Peacoat and skirt in silk jersey by Racine Byzance. Straw hat with grosgrain ribbon. Twill scarf. Silk satin sandals.
Made to order for HRH The Duchess of Windsor.

29
Daytime Ensemble
Spring–Summer 1962
Duffle coat in wool by Prud'homme. T-shirt and shantung pants by Pétillault. Metal stud earrings. Leather mules.
Metropolitan Museum of Art, New York, 1983. Palace of Fine Arts, Beijing, 1985. Musée des Arts de la Mode, Paris, 1986. Tretyakov Gallery, Moscow, 1986. State Hermitage Museum, St. Petersburg, 1987. Art Gallery, Sydney, 1987. Sezon Museum of Art, Tokyo, 1990. Musée de la Mode, Marseille, 1993.
Publications
Observer, United States, June 5, 1977.
Paris Match, France, December 4, 1981.
Elle, France, January 27, 1992.

30
Evening Ensemble
Fall–Winter 1962
Norman blouse in satin and skirt in velvet by Brossin de Méré. Velvet overstitching. Snakeskin, metal, and faceted jet stud earrings. Metal and colored bead pin. Suede gloves and pumps.
Metropolitan Museum of Art, New York, 1983. Palace of Fine Arts, Beijing, 1985. Musée des Arts de la Mode, Paris, 1986. Tretyakov Gallery, Moscow, 1986. State Hermitage Museum, St. Petersburg, 1987. Art Gallery, Sydney, 1987. Sezon Museum of Art, Tokyo, 1990.
Publications
Vogue, United States, 1962.
Harper's Bazaar, United States, September 1962.
Vogue, United States, September 15, 1962.
Vogue, France, November 1962.

31
Cocktail Dress
Spring–Summer 1966
Sequin embroidery by Malhia. Leather sandals.

32
Skirtsuit
Fall–Winter 1967
Wool jersey by Racine Paris Midi and metal belt. Fur, leather, and metal cap. Suede moccasins.
Made to order for Françoise Giroud.
Musée des Arts de la Mode, Paris, 1986.

33
Daytime Ensemble
July 1968
Safari jacket and Bermuda shorts in cotton gabardine by Aquaviva. Suede hat. Rope and metal stud earrings. Metal ring belt. Suede and leather boots.
Special commission for *Vogue,* France.
Metropolitan Museum of Art, New York, 1983. Palace of Fine Arts, Beijing, 1985. Musée des Arts de la Mode, Paris, 1986. Tretyakov Gallery, Moscow, 1986. State Hermitage Museum, St. Petersburg, 1987. Art Gallery, Sydney, 1987. Sezon Museum of Art, Tokyo, 1990. Musée de la Mode, Marseille, 1993. Fondation Pierre Bergé–Yves Saint Laurent, Paris, 2006.
Publications
Vogue (cover), France, 1968.
Paris Match, France, December 4, 1981.
Elle, France, January 27, 1992.
Vogue, Spain, April 2001.

34
Jumpsuit
Fall–Winter 1969
Wool jersey by Racine Byzance. Patent leather pumps with metal buckles.
Made to order for Nan Kempner.
Fondation Pierre Bergé–Yves Saint Laurent, Paris, 2007.

35
Trench Coat
Fall–Winter 1995
Satin. Metal necklace. Satin pumps.

36
Daytime Ensemble
Fall–Winter 1963
Tunic with suede cagoule. Woolen hose. Suede gloves. Thigh boots.
Made to order for Niki de Saint-Phalle.
Metropolitan Museum of Art, New York, 1983. Musée des Arts de la Mode, Paris, 1986. Tretyakov Gallery, Moscow, 1986. State Hermitage Museum, St. Petersburg, 1987. Art Gallery, Sydney, 1987.

37
Day Dress
Fall–Winter 1970
Thick wool jersey by Racine. Knitted cap. Leather boots.
Made to order for Zizi Jeanmaire, Nan Kempner, and Madeleine Renaud.
Fondation Pierre Bergé–Yves Saint Laurent, Paris, 2007.

38
Daytime Ensemble
Spring–Summer 1971
Blazer in woolen gabardine by Dormeuil. Shorts in woolen gabardine by Perceval. Sandals of composite patent leather. Ensemble made to order for Betty Catroux. Blazer made to order for Catherine Deneuve.
Publications
Marie-Claire, France, March 1971.
L'Officiel, France, April 1971.
Harper's & Queen, United Kingdom, February 1971.

39
Daytime Ensemble
Fall–Winter 2000
Woolen jersey tunic by Gandini. Leather skirt by Sonia. Fox-fur wrap. Felt and taffeta hat. Leather gloves. Agate and faceted cabochon stud earrings. Leather and suede ghillie shoes.

40
Evening Ensemble
Fall–Winter 1984
Velvet blouson by Moreau. "YSL" embroidery by Lanel. Barathea pants. Velvet and rhinestone turban. Rhinestone, metal, and faceted cabochon stud earrings. Silk satin pumps.
Made to order for Betty Catroux.

AN AMBIGUOUS ATTRACTION

"AT THE TIME, WOMEN HAD A PARTICULAR ATTRACTION, PERHAPS BECAUSE OF THE UNCERTAINTY OF THE CLIMATE OF MEN, DREAMS, AND HEROES."

Yves Saint Laurent talking about his 1971 collection, quoted by Laurence Benaïm, in *Yves Saint Laurent* (Paris: Grasset, 1993), p. 208, interviewed in 1986.

The famous summer collection of 1971 was a shock tactic at the height of the hippie and feminist movements. It awoke the buried memories of the War and revived the past in a sophistication that reeked of sulfur. The seductress seen through the filter of history abandons herself to forbidden romance. In *Belle de jour,* Catherine Deneuve hides her fiery temperament beneath the modest dress of an ingenue. Coquettishness, according to Yves Saint Laurent, consists of extremes, prudery, or teasing, sometimes expressing indifference, sometimes passion in sexy dresses draped over the hips or a sparkling bustier for nightclub wear. In 1968, Nan Kempner was stopped from entering a restaurant because she had dared to arrive in an eveningwear pantsuit. She did not hesitate for a moment, taking off her pants and keeping on her tunic, which had now become an ultra-miniskirt. The little-girl style in a black-and-white gym slip was rivaled by the outside-inside spirit of lingerie in the form of corsets or panty-girdles worn externally as part of a dress.

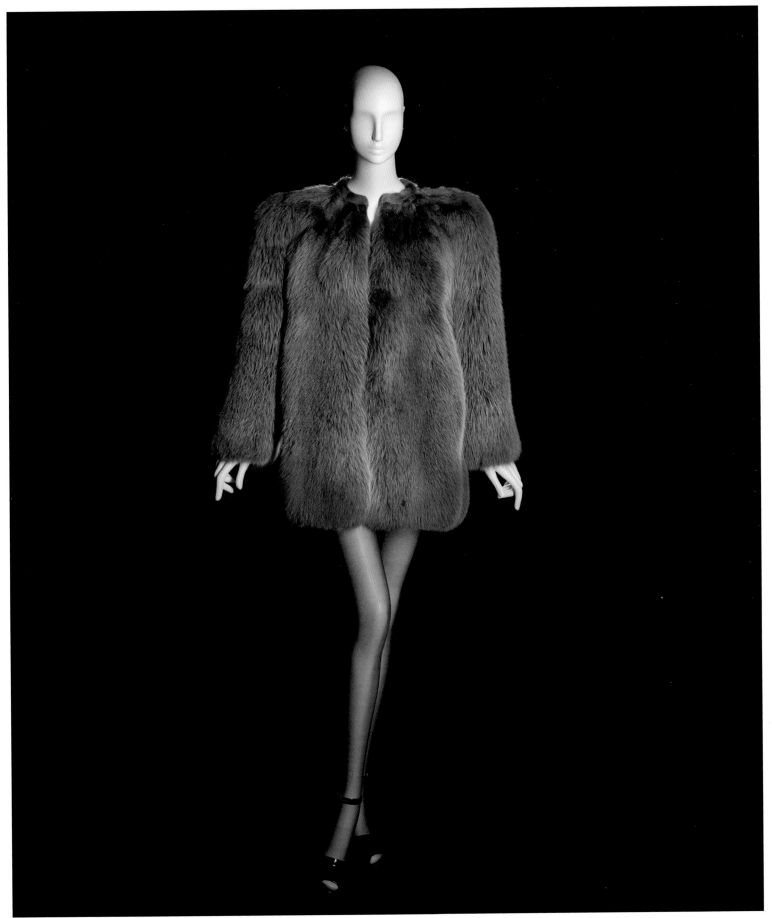

5031   Simone

sur

Olla

20

Leleu

6225 noir

plastron lingerie
Allaman

H/amon ceinture vernis
noir 8567 ½ cm plus large

avec manteau 5169

1ère annulée
Scemama
2/ 1 paire boutons de manchette
R/2525/12

73

4108.

Blanche
Valérie

Abraham
5315/60

Col et poignets
de satin blanc.
Abraham 5315 col Bl.
Barbier
1 Camélias Scenamama
8 Pts Satin noir 2448/18
1 paire BM Satin et
perle Bl.

67

43

45

46_1

46_2

47
Esther

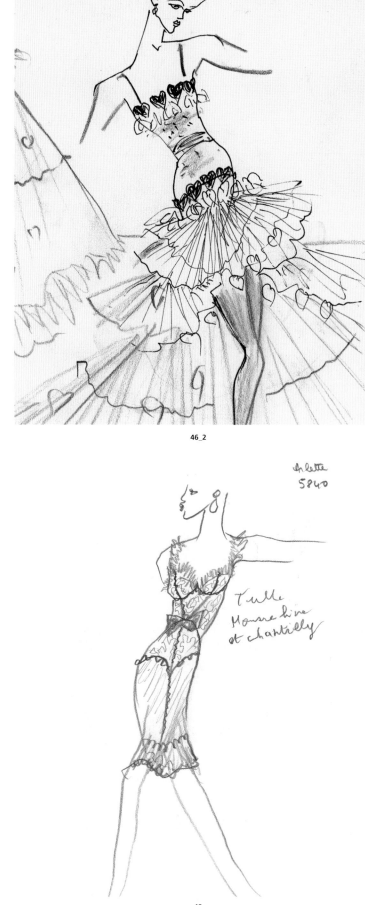

48
Arlette
5840

Tulle
Mousseline
et chantilly

2103.
2104

49

41
Evening Coat
Spring–Summer 1971
Fox fur. Patent leather sandals.
Metropolitan Museum of Art, New York, 1983. Palace of
Fine Arts, Beijing, 1985. Musée des Arts de la Mode, Paris,
1986. Art Gallery, Sydney, 1987. Sezon Museum of Art,
Tokyo, 1990.
Publications
Vogue, United States, March 15, 1971.
Vogue, France, March 1971.
Elle, France, March 1, 1971.
Newsweek, United States, March 29, 1971.

42
Day Dress
Fall–Winter 1966
Patterned woolen fabric by Leleu. Plastron
and cuffs in organdie by Allaman. Satin
bow. Metal and colored bead cuff buttons.
Colored bead stud earrings. Patent leather
belt by Hamon. Lamé pantyhose. Patent
leather pumps with buckles designed by
Yves Saint Laurent and made by Roger Vivier.
Made to order for Claude Lalanne.
Publication
Glamour, United States, April 1967.

43
Evening Ensemble
Fall–Winter 1968
Tunic, pants, belt in silk satin with trimming.
Collar and cuffs in silk satin. Colored bead
and jet stud earrings. Colored bead and jet
cuff buttons. Satin ankle boots.
Made to order for Jane Fonda, Nan Kempner,
Hélène Rochas, and Diana Vreeland.
Fondation Pierre Bergé–Yves Saint Laurent, Paris, 2007.
Publication
Vogue, United States, September 1, 1968.

44
Silk Coat
Spring–Summer 1971
Velvet by Rodolphe Simon. "Lips" embroidery
by Mesrine. Rhinestone and metal bracelets.
Patent leather platform sandals.
Made to order for Marisa Berenson.
Musée des Arts de la Mode, Paris, 1986. Art Gallery,
Sydney, 1987.
Publication
Elle, France, March 1, 1971.

45
Day Dress
Spring–Summer 1971
Silk jersey by Racine Parthénon. Rhinestone
and metal pendant on a satin ribbon. Patent
leather platform sandals.
Publication
Vogue, United States, March 15, 1971.

46_1, 46_2
Evening Gown
Spring–Summer 1980
Tulle and point d'esprit by Hurel. "Heart"
embroidery by Lisbeth. Silk satin ribbon belt.
Metal leaf pendant earrings. Colored bead
necklace. Guipure lace gloves. Rhinestone
and metal cuffs. Sandals with satin bow.
Musée des Arts de la Mode, 1986, Paris.
Publication
Vogue, France, January 3, 1980.

47
Evening Gown
Fall–Winter 1981
Silk taffeta by Guillaud. Rhinestone and
metal stud earrings and cuffs. Painted silk
feather and sequins by Nina Wood. Satin and
rhinestone pumps.
Metropolitan Museum of Art, New York, 1983. Palace
of Fine Arts, Beijing, 1985. Sezon Museum of Art,
Tokyo, 1990.

48
Evening Gown
Fall–Winter 1991
Lacquered lace by Marescot. Ribbed crêpe by
Taroni. Velvet by Rodolphe Simon. Metal and
colored bead pendant earrings by Goossens.
Lace pumps.
Musée de la Mode, Marseille, 1993.
Publication
Vogue, France, September 1991.

49
Evening Gown
Spring–Summer 1971
Silk crêpe "camouflage" print by Abraham.
Fox wrap by Pelletier. Silk flower by
Fromentin. Patent leather sandals.
Metropolitan Museum of Art, New York, 1983. Musée des
Arts de la Mode, Paris, 1986.
Publication
Vogue, Italy, June 1971.

50
"Belle de Jour" Dress
Barathea. Collar and cuffs in silk satin. Patent
leather belt. Colored bead, rhinestone, and
metal cuff buttons. Leather pumps.
Worn by Catherine Deneuve in *Belle de jour,*
the movie directed by Luis Buñuel in 1967.
Musée des Arts de la Mode, Paris, 1986. Fondation Pierre
Bergé–Yves Saint Laurent, Paris, 2007.

FUNDAMENTALS FOR THE EVENING

"IT IS BY PERFECTING ESSENTIAL ITEMS OF CLOTHING—A MARVELOUS POSITION—THAT I CREATED MY STYLE, THAT I BECAME WHAT I AM, AND THROUGH THIS, I OVERTAKE FASHION."

Yves Saint Laurent, quoted by Laurence Benaïm, in *Yves Saint Laurent*, op. cit., p. 318.

The bases for the modern wardrobe, peacoat, safari suit, or tuxedo are what construct the codes of the house of Yves Saint Laurent. Their fundamental importance in the brand identity lends themselves to all sorts of interpretations, thus demolishing the traditional opposition between day and night. In the evening version, the tuxedo adopts the shocking transparency of a blouse showing the bust naked under black muslin. Above and beyond the shock effect, Yves Saint Laurent produces an apology for the beauty of skin, veiled in silk, and dedicated to nudity in his collection for summer 1999. A "Marcel" tank top transformed by black-sequined embroidery is impudently matched with an elegant suit. Gold-and-silver embroidery imitate the braided pattern of Arran sweaters, or the irregular surface of tweed is reproduced in bugle beads and sequins. The duffle coat is revisited in silk gazar or Bermuda shorts in barathea, worn gracefully in the evening.

53

55

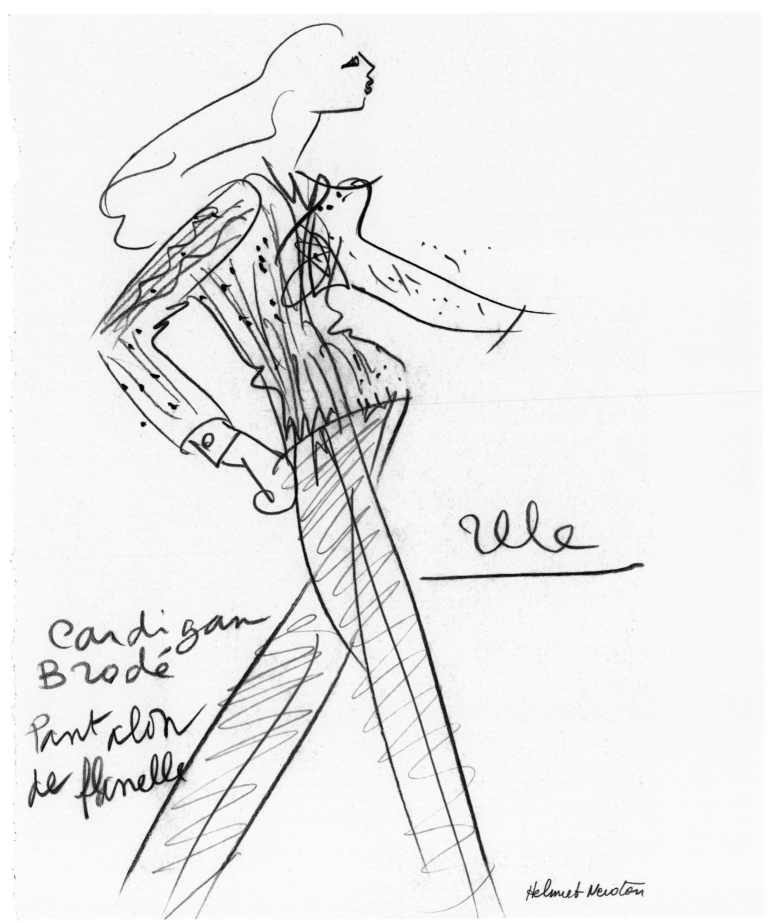

Cardigan
Brodé

Pantalon
de flanelle

Helmut Newton

57

51
Premier Tuxedo
Fall–Winter 1966
Jacket and pants in barathea and silk satin
by Dormeuil. Cambric blouse. Bow and waist
draped in satin. Colored bead, jet, and metal
sleeve buttons. Satin silk ankle boots.
Made to order for Françoise Hardy and
Lady Smith.
Metropolitan Museum of Art, New York, 1983. Palace of
Fine Arts, Beijing, 1985. Tretyakov Gallery, Moscow, 1986.
State Hermitage Museum, St. Petersburg, 1987. Art
Gallery, Sydney, 1987. Fondation Pierre Bergé–Yves Saint
Laurent, Paris, 2005.
Publications
Vogue, France, September 1966.
Vogue, France, December 1966.
Glamour, United States, April 1967.

52
Evening Ensemble
Fall–Winter 1967
Tunic in calf velour by Cuvreau with sleeves
of sequined mesh by Marescot. Skirt in wool
jersey by Racine. Metal stud earrings and
belt. Calf velour pumps.
Made to order for Bettina Graziani, Princess
Lee Radziwill, and HRH The Duchess of
Windsor.
Art Gallery, Sydney, 1987.
Publication
L'Officiel, France, September 1, 1967.

53
Evening Gown
Fall–Winter 1968
Silk muslin by Bianchini. Ostrich feathers by
Barbier. Metal snake belt by Denez. Pumps
with patent leather straps.
Metropolitan Museum of Art, New York, 1983. Palace of
Fine Arts, Beijing, 1985. Musée des Arts de la Mode, Paris,
1986. Tretyakov Gallery, Moscow, 1986. State Hermitage
Museum, St. Petersburg, 1987. Art Gallery, Sydney, 1987.
Sezon Museum of Art, Tokyo, 1990. Musée de la Mode,
Marseille, 1993.
Publications
Vogue, France, March 1968.
Vogue, United Kingdom, September 1968.
City, France, May 1988.
Madame Figaro, France, June 1994.

54
Tuxedo
Spring–Summer 1970
Full-length dress of crêpe sheeting and silk
satin by Abraham. Plastic and rhinestone
bracelet. Leather pumps.
Musée des Arts de la Mode, Paris, 1986. Musée de la
Mode, Marseille, 1993.
Publication
Vogue, France, March 1, 1970.

55
Tuxedo
Fall–Winter 1999
Muslin tank top with sequin by Schlaepfer.
Silk satin corded trim by Helsa. Full-length
skirt in crêpe sheeting by Bianchini. Stone
and metal pendant earrings. Satin pumps.

56
Evening Ensemble
Fall–Winter 1973
Cardigan, sequin, bugle bead, and stone
embroidery by Lesage. Blouse with
cheesecloth lavallière cravat by Bianchini.
Pants in flannel by Gandini. Satin pumps.
Made to order for Lauren Bacall, Betty
Catroux, Catherine Deneuve, and
Françoise Giroud.
Metropolitan Museum of Art, New York, 1983. Musée des
Arts de la Mode, Paris, 1986. Tretyakov Gallery, Moscow,
1986. State Hermitage Museum, St. Petersburg, 1987.

57
Tuxedo
Fall–Winter 1991
Jacket, vest, and pants in barathea by
Dormeuil. Silk grosgrain by Bucol. Silk muslin
scarf by Gandini. Stud earrings in wood,
rhinestone, and metal. Silk satin sandals.
Fondation Pierre Bergé–Yves Saint Laurent, Paris, 2005.
Publication
Marie Claire, France, September 1991.

58
Tuxedo
Spring–Summer 1968
Jacket and Bermuda shorts in barathea and
silk satin by Dormeuil. Blouse in Cigaline
muslin by Bucol. Satin by Dormeuil. Jet,
metal, and colored bead stud earrings.
Glazed cotton flower. Belt and strappy
pumps in patent leather.
Metropolitan Museum of Art, New York, 1983. Palace of
Fine Arts, Beijing, 1985. Musée des Arts de la Mode, Paris,
1986. Tretyakov Gallery, Moscow, 1986. State Hermitage
Museum, St. Petersburg, 1987. Art Gallery, Sydney, 1987.
Sezon Museum of Art, Tokyo, 1990. Musée de la Mode,
Marseille, 1993. Fondation Pierre Bergé–Yves Saint
Laurent, Paris, 2005.
Publications
Vogue, France, March 1968.
Vogue, United States, March 15, 1968.
L'Officiel, France, March 1968.
Vogue, United Kingdom, March 1968.

THE
PALETTE

Yves Saint Laurent is a creator who, like his predecessors Paul Poiret and Elsa Schiaparelli, has dared to use color by scoffing at the traditional rules in the history of haute couture. In principle, a couturier chooses colors that go well with the color scheme and do not risk appearing to clash. But Saint Laurent very freely chose his fabrics by composing a painter's palette. His preferences veer toward red, pink, and black, and unexpected combinations such as blue and black. Known for his extended and daring register of colors, Saint Laurent nevertheless maintains a passion for black, his favorite color for daywear. He avoids the brilliance of colors in sunshine, preferring neutral shades, and reserving them for the penumbra of the salons, the mysteries of the night, the spells cast by the evening.

MOROCCO

"ON EACH STREET CORNER IN MARRAKECH,
YOU ENCOUNTER GROUPS THAT ARE IMPRESSIVE
IN THEIR INTENSITY, THEIR RELIEF. MEN AND
WOMEN, WHERE PINK, BLUE, GREEN, AND VIOLET
CAFTANS MINGLE. THESE GROUPS LOOK AS IF
THEY HAVE BEEN DRAWN AND PAINTED, THAT
ARE REMINISCENT OF SKETCHES BY DELACROIX,
AND IT IS SURPRISING TO SAY THAT THEY ARE,
IN FACT, MERELY AN IMPROVISATION ON LIFE."

Yves Saint Laurent, quoted by Laurence Benaïm, in *Yves Saint Laurent* (Paris: Grasset, 1993), p. 261.

The first collections were dominated by a somber or monochrome color scheme. When he discovered Morocco, Yves Saint Laurent rediscovered the bright hues of his childhood. His talents as a colorist exploded in his sketches with their violent and authentic shades of ocher, sand, earth, and azure. The sight of women relaxing on a beach, protected from the sun by brightly colored cloths and a mixture of patterns, had a shock effect on him. His passion for Marrakech stems in part from the exceptional color and light of this city. The burnous-style capes of 1969, the veil that was the theme of summer 1988, the cape embroidered with bougainvillea in 1989 are examples of the richness of his Moroccan palette. The homage to Bakst offers an expanded vision of a mythical Orient.

60

4407 J·M
gazar violet

61_1

100

Galy 4404

61_2

59
Evening Ensemble
Fall–Winter 1969
Cape in homespun by Daure. Trimming by
Denez. Georgette crêpe dress and leather
and metal belt. Metal necklace and bracelet.
Metal and mother-of-pearl pendant earrings.
Wool jersey turban. Satin sandals.
Cape made to order for Lauren Bacall,
Catherine Deneuve, and Nan Kempner.
Metropolitan Museum of Art, New York, 1983. Musée des
Arts de la Mode, Paris, 1986. Fondation Pierre Bergé–Yves
Saint Laurent, Paris, 2006.

60
Evening Ensemble
Spring–Summer 1988
Poncho, dress, belt, and turban in muslin by
Bianchini. Satin sandals.
Made to order for Nan Kempner.
Musée de la Mode, Marseille, 1993. Fondation Pierre
Bergé–Yves Saint Laurent, Paris, 2006.

61_1, 61_2
Evening Ensemble
Spring–Summer 1989
Cape in silk gazar by Abraham.
"Bougainvillea" embroidery by Lesage. Dress
and muslin belt by Saris. Ceramic, colored
bead, faceted cabochon, and metal earrings.
Satin pumps.
Fondation Pierre Bergé–Yves Saint Laurent, Paris, 2006.
Publication
Town & Country, United States, June 1, 1989.

62
**Evening Ensemble in Tribute to
Leon Bakst**
Spring–Summer 1991
Cheesecloth harem pants. Organdie stole.
Glass beaded top. Passementerie hat. Enamel
pendant earrings. Wooden beads and metal
bracelets. Passementerie belt and enamel
bead, paste gem, and metal pin. Leather
sandals and trimming.
Musée de la Mode, Marseille, 1993. Fondation Pierre
Bergé–Yves Saint Laurent, Paris, 2006.
Publication
Harper's Bazaar, Germany, January 1991.

IMAGINARY VOYAGES

"I AM VERY ALONE. I EXERCISE MY IMAGINATION ON THE LANDS THAT I DO NOT KNOW. I HATE TRAVELING. FOR EXAMPLE, IF I READ A BOOK ABOUT INDIA, WITH PHOTOGRAPHS, OR ABOUT EGYPT, WHERE I HAVE NEVER BEEN, MY IMAGINATION RUNS WILD. THAT IS HOW I TAKE MY MOST WONDERFUL TRIPS. PUTTING MY IMAGINATION TO WORK IS VALUABLE TO ME. FROM *WOMAN WITH A PEARL NECKLACE* BY VERMEER, I IMAGINED THE DRESS SHE MIGHT HAVE BEEN WEARING. AND I THINK IT IS ONE OF THE MOST BEAUTIFUL DRESSES I EVER CREATED."

Interview with Catherine Deneuve, *Globe,* France, May 1, 1986.

Most couturiers, when lacking inspiration, undertake trips to distant places to rediscover their muse. Yves Saint Laurent rejects this way of working. The images of distant lands are sufficient to get his imagination working, and leaving him more freedom to evoke what lies elsewhere as the mood takes him. Between Russia and Spain, Japan, India and China, his allusions meet, merge, and weave new links that resist any anthropological analysis. The Russian collection revived the concept of sumptuousness in fashion in 1976. The Spanish women of 1977 dressed like dogaresses, in gypsy skirts, or velvet corselettes in the style of Carmen, Chinese women in imperial robes or perfumed with Opium (the perfume released in that year), Mandarins in kimonos in 1994, as well as Indian women in 1969 and 1982 are spectacular evidence of these imaginary voyages.

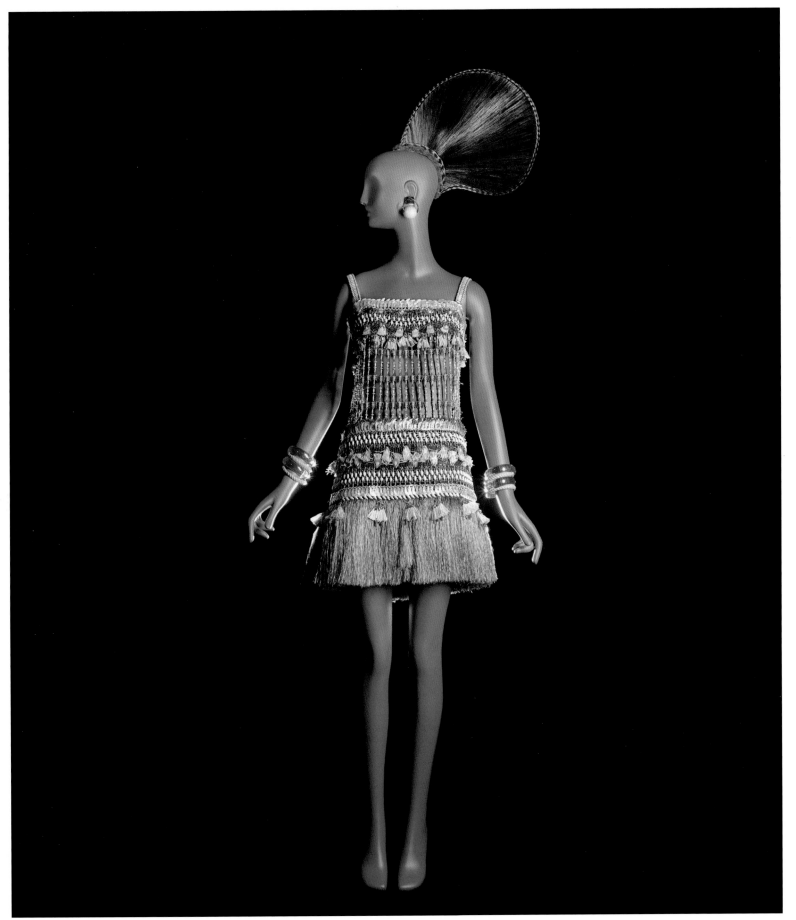

Soir Co

SoiR - LO

63   68   67   66   65_1

65_2

(Not exhibited)

64_3

"PEKING, HOWEVER, REMAINS A DAZZLING MEMORY. THIS CHINA THAT I HAVE SO OFTEN INTERPRETED IN MY CREATIONS, I FOUND TO BE EXACTLY AS I HAD IMAGINED IT. ALL I NEED IS A PICTURE BOOK FOR MY MIND TO MELT INTO A PLACE OR A LANDSCAPE. I ONLY KNOW EGYPT THROUGH PHOTOGRAPHS. I DON'T FEEL ANY NEED TO GO THERE. I HAVE DREAMED ABOUT IT SO MUCH. . . . IN THE END, THE MOST WONDERFUL VOYAGE IS THE ONE THAT ONE TAKES AROUND ONE'S ROOM."

Yves Saint Laurent, *Elle*, France, December 25, 1995.

69

70

tunique
Abraham
3692/83
bordée du 89
Knickers satin
vert foncé
3692/67
Broderie soie Negrines.

6478
J.Pierre

73

74

77

7808
TP
7808 bis
7808 ter

79

81

126

Soir

AH76-77-

Blanche

Catherine

83

Esther

80_1

85

84

9086.

Après Blanche
s/ Kira. **67**

Robe soir long.

Haut de velours noir.
Leonard 1186 2 cf Nr.

Manches de satin orange.
Abraham. 8600 col 7.

Cape de satin turquoise
Taroni 2569 col 6

Ruban satin fushia ceinture
Ruban velours Bordeaux

N° 96
Châle : Lamé or / violet / bleu fuschia
Lamé.
BO rubis / émeraude

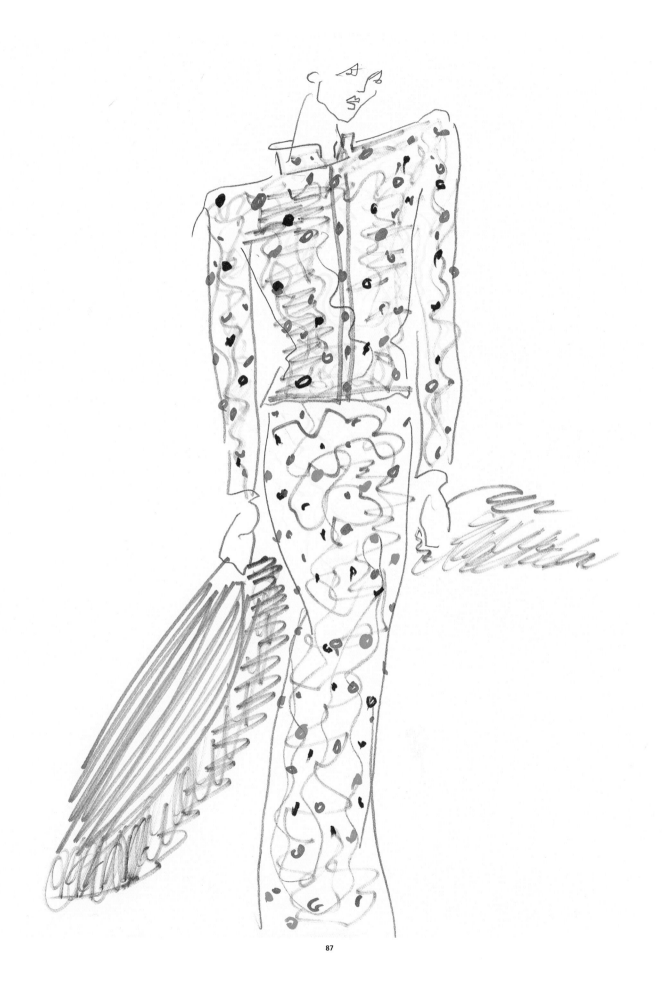

87

106
mussel

2572

Felisa / Kiat
Robe longue en
panne de velours
noir et or
Abraham 9004-82
col 260

- BO clips papillons or Goossens
  (1 grand + 1 petit)
- collier nombreux rangs
  de médailles or Goossens

- 2 manchettes découpées
  or - Roux -

PM 10/7

89

63
Evening Gown
Spring–Summer 1967
Embroidery by Rhodoïd. Wooden beads by Lanel. Wood and metal pendant earrings. Plastic cord and wooden beads. Hair by Alexandre of Paris.

Metropolitan Museum of Art, New York, 1983. Palace of Fine Arts, Beijing, 1985. Musée des Arts de la Mode, Paris, 1986. Tretyakov Gallery, Moscow, 1986. State Hermitage Museum, St. Petersburg, 1987. Art Gallery, Sydney, 1987. Fondation Pierre Bergé–Yves Saint Laurent, Paris, 2004.
Publication
WWD, United States, January 1967.

64_1, 64_2, 64_3
Evening Gown
Spring–Summer 1967
Embroidery by Rhodoïd. Wood and copper beads by Lanel. Pendant wood and metal earrings with plastic bangles. Wooden beaded ankle bracelet. Hair by Alexandre of Paris.
Made to order for Baroness Van Zuylen.

Metropolitan Museum of Art, New York, 1983. Palace of Fine Arts, Beijing, 1985. Tretyakov Gallery, Moscow, 1986. State Hermitage Museum, St. Petersburg, 1987. Art Gallery, Sydney, 1987. Musée de la Mode, Marseille, 1993. Fondation Pierre Bergé–Yves Saint Laurent, Paris, 2004 and 2006.
Publications
Vogue, United States, March 1967.
L'Officiel, France, March 1967.
Vogue, United States, November 1967.

65_1, 65_2
"Bambara" Dress
Spring–Summer 1967
Wooden bead and raffia embroidery by Lanel. Metal and wood pendant earrings. Wooden bead and raffia cuffs. Wooden bangle. Hair by Alexandre of Paris.

Metropolitan Museum of Art, New York, 1983. Palace of Fine Arts, Beijing, 1985. Tretyakov Gallery, Moscow, 1986. State Hermitage Museum, St. Petersburg, 1987. Art Gallery, Sydney, 1987. Fondation Pierre Bergé–Yves Saint Laurent, Paris, 2004 and 2006.

66
"Tropical" Dress
Spring–Summer 1967
Wooden bead Rhodoïd and raffia embroidery by Lanel. Skirt in silk twill by Abraham. Metal, wood, and raffia pendant earrings with plastic bangles. Hair by Alexandre of Paris.

Metropolitan Museum of Art, New York, 1983. Palace of Fine Arts, Beijing, 1987. Musée des Arts de la Mode, Paris, 1986. Tretyakov Gallery, Moscow, 1986. State Hermitage Museum, St. Petersburg, 1987. Art Gallery, Sydney, 1987. Fondation Pierre Bergé–Yves Saint Laurent, Paris, 2006.

67
"Tropical" Dress
Spring–Summer 1967
Wooden bead and Rhodoïd embroidery by Lanel. Skirt in silk twill by Abraham. Metal and wood pendant earrings with plastic bangles. Hair by Alexandre of Paris.

Metropolitan Museum of Art, New York, 1983. Palace of Fine Arts, Beijing, 1985. Musée des Arts de la Mode, Paris, 1986. Tretyakov Gallery, Moscow, 1986. State Hermitage Museum, St. Petersburg, 1987. Art Gallery, Sydney, 1987. Musée de la Mode, Marseille, 1993. Fondation Pierre Bergé–Yves Saint Laurent, Paris, 2006.

68
"Tropical" Dress
Spring–Summer 1967
Wooden bead Rhodoïd and raffia embroidery by Lanel. Skirt in silk twill by Abraham. Metal and wood pendant earrings with plastic bangles. Wooden beads choker. Hair by Alexandre of Paris.

Metropolitan Museum of Art, New York, 1983. Palace of Fine Arts, Beijing, 1985. Musée des Arts de la Mode, Paris, 1986. Tretyakov Gallery, Moscow, 1986. State Hermitage Museum, St. Petersburg, 1987. Art Gallery, Sydney, 1987. Fondation Pierre Bergé–Yves Saint Laurent, Paris, 2006.

69
Evening Ensemble
Fall–Winter 1977
Great-coat in quilted ciré by Pennel. Trimming by Leroux. Velvet pants by Chatillon. Ciré, velvet, and feather hat. Passementerie and metal pendant earrings. Passementerie belt. Leather and fur gloves. Suede, mink, and passementerie boots.

Metropolitan Museum of Art, New York, 1983. Palace of Fine Arts, Beijing, 1985. Musée des Arts de la Mode, Paris, 1986. Tretyakov Gallery, Moscow, 1986. State Hermitage Museum, St. Petersburg, 1987. Art Gallery, Sydney, 1987. Sezon Museum of Art, Tokyo, 1990. Fondation Pierre Bergé–Yves Saint Laurent, Paris, 2006.

70
Evening Ensemble
Fall–Winter 1977
Damascene great-coat by Abraham. Fox-fur cuffs. Pants in oversewn velvet by Chatillon. Knotted ciré hairband. Metal pendant earrings. Leather and fur gloves. Trimmed suede boots.

Metropolitan Museum of Art, New York, 1983. Palace of Fine Arts, Beijing, 1985. Musée des Arts de la Mode, Paris, 1986. Tretyakov Gallery, Moscow, 1986. State Hermitage Museum, St. Petersburg, 1987. Art Gallery, Sydney, 1987. Musée de la Mode, Marseille, 1993. Fondation Pierre Bergé–Yves Saint Laurent, Paris, 2006.
Publication
Madame Figaro, France, October 28, 1988.

71
"Opium" Evening Ensemble
Fall–Winter 1977
Ciré fabric. Sequin embroidery. Corduroy and passementerie pants. Passementerie and plastic necklace. Metal pendant earrings. Ciré hat. Leather gloves and pumps.

Fondation Pierre Bergé–Yves Saint Laurent, Paris, 2006.

72
Evening Ensemble
Fall–Winter 1970
Tunic and pants in satin by Abraham. Embroidery by Mesrine. Velvet belt by Bianchini. Metal and stone buckle by Péral. Suede boots.

Fondation Pierre Bergé–Yves Saint Laurent, Paris, 2006.
Publication
Vogue, France, September 1970.

73
Evening Ensemble
Fall–Winter 1994
Mandarin coat in quilted silk by Abraham. Beaded trimming by Leroux. Dress in muslin by Abraham. Metal pendant earrings and bracelet by Goossens. Satin and metal sandals.

Fondation Pierre Bergé–Yves Saint Laurent, Paris, 2006.

74
Evening Gown
Spring–Summer 1977
Silk gazar by Abraham. Velvet by Léonard. Tulle pompons by Fromentin. Satin ribbon belt by Guillemin. Tulle veil. Silk flower. Jet pendant earrings and crystal necklace by Labeyre. Satin pumps with leather edging and laces.

Musée des Arts de la Mode, Paris, 1986.

75
Evening Ensemble
Spring–Summer 1977
Muslin netting blouse by Bucol. Figured and striped muslin skirt by Abraham. Satin ribbon by Rodolphe Simon. Colored bead, passementerie, and glass pendant earrings and necklace. Braided leather sandals.
Made to order for Marisa Berenson.
Publication
L'Officiel, France, March 1, 1977.

76
Cocktail Ensemble
Spring–Summer 1977
Corselette in moiré faille by Taroni. Cotton Bermuda shorts. Shawl by Hurel. Passementerie and metal pendant earrings, necklace, and bracelets. Silk flower. Satin sandals with leather edging and laces.

Metropolitan Museum of Art, New York, 1983. Palace of Fine Arts, Beijing, 1985. Musée des Arts de la Mode, Paris, 1986. Tretyakov Gallery, Moscow, 1986. State Hermitage Museum, St. Petersburg, 1987. Art Gallery, Sydney, 1987. Fondation Pierre Bergé–Yves Saint Laurent, Paris, 2006.
Publication
WWD, United States, October 22, 1976

77
Toreador Costume
Fall–Winter 1979
Lamé brocade by Abraham. Velvet by Léonard. Satin pompon and ribbon trimming. Blouse in muslin by Gandini. Satin jabot and ribbon by Lemarié. Passementerie belt. Satin and velvet hat. Metal and rhinestone pendant earrings. Satin sandals with leather edging and laces.

Metropolitan Museum of Art, New York, 1983. Musée des Arts de la Mode, Paris, 1986. Tretyakov Gallery, Moscow, 1986. State Hermitage Museum, St. Petersburg, 1987. Art Gallery, Sydney, 1987.

78
Evening Gown
Fall–Winter 1979
Cape in silk gazar by Abraham. Velvet by Hurel. Trimming by Leroux. Dress in velvet by Bianchini. Silk gazar by Abraham. Butterfly by Nina Wood. Rhinestone and metal bracelets. Pearl and passementerie necklace. Satin sandals with leather laces with pompons.

Metropolitan Museum of Art, New York, 1983. Palace of Fine Arts, Beijing, 1985. Musée des Arts de la Mode, Paris, 1986. Tretyakov Gallery, Moscow, 1986. State Hermitage Museum, St. Petersburg, 1987. Art Gallery, Sydney, 1987. Fondation Pierre Bergé–Yves Saint Laurent, Paris, 2006.
Publication
Vogue, United States, October 1979.

79
Day Ensemble
Fall–Winter 2000
Bolero in wool and cashmere by Dormeuil. Waistcoat in velvet by Moreau. Crêpe satin edge by Buche. High-waisted pants in flannel by Holland & Sherry. Felt, leather, and velvet hat. Agate and rhinestone cabochon earrings by Goossens. Suede gloves. Leather and suede pumps with leather laces.

80_1, 80_2
Evening Gown
Fall–Winter 1976
Top in velvet by Léonard. Sleeves in satin by Abraham. Skirt in satin by Taroni edged with velvet ribbon by Rodolphe Simon. Satin ribbon belt. Printed crushed velvet turban. Shawl in lamé muslin by Abraham with fringes by Leroux. Stone and metal pendant earrings. Metal and rhinestone cuffs. Leather sandals.

Metropolitan Museum of Art, New York, 1983. Palace of Fine Arts, Beijing, 1985. Musée des Arts de la Mode, Paris, 1986. Tretyakov Gallery, Moscow, 1986. State Hermitage Museum, St. Petersburg, 1987. Art Gallery, Sydney, 1987. Sezon Museum of Art, Tokyo, 1990. Fondation Pierre Bergé–Yves Saint Laurent, Paris, 2006.
Publications
Time, United States, August 9, 1976.
Vogue, United States, October 1976.

81
Daytime Ensemble
Fall–Winter 1976
Coat in homespun with corded trimming
by Besson. Blouse in loose-weave wool by
Staron. Skirt in wool by Moreau. Suede
by Hamon. Suede skull-cap by Poulain edged
with fox fur by Garande and trimming.
Loose-weave wool shawl. Leather gloves.
Suede boots.
Metropolitan Museum of Art, New York, 1983. Palace of
Fine Arts, Beijing, 1985. Musée des Arts de la Mode, Paris,
1986. Art Gallery, Sydney, 1987. Fondation Pierre
Bergé–Yves Saint Laurent, Paris, 2006.
Publication
Time, United States, August 9, 1976.

82
Daytime Ensemble
Fall–Winter 1976
Suede pelisse by Curreau embroidered
and lined with fur by Garande. Tunic of
loose-woven wool by Staron. Embroidery by
Lesage. Trimming by Leroux. Worsted skirt
by Moreau. Suede belt and gloves. Loose-
woven wool scarf. Mink toque. Suede and
leather boots.
Skirt and tunic made to order for Hélène
Rochas.
Metropolitan Museum of Art, New York, 1983. Palace of
Fine Arts, Beijing, 1985. Musée des Arts de la Mode, Paris,
1986. Fondation Pierre Bergé–Yves Saint Laurent, Paris,
2006.

83
Evening Ensemble
Fall–Winter 1976
Vest in velvet by Gandini. Sable by Garande.
Blouse in lamé muslin by Bianchini. Trimming
by Leroux. Skirt in silk faille by Abraham.
Velvet ribbon by Rodolphe Simon. Passe-
menterie by Hamon, velvet, and rhinestone
belt. Lamé silk muslin shawl by Abraham.
Pheasant plumes. Fringes by Leroux. Turban
in panné velvet by Abraham. Colored beads,
rhinestone, and metal pendant earrings.
Velvet, metal, and rhinestone cuffs.
Snakeskin pumps.
Metropolitan Museum of Art, New York, 1983. Palace of
Fine Arts, Beijing, 1985. Musée des Arts de la Mode, Paris,
1986. Tretyakov Gallery, Moscow, 1986. State Hermitage
Museum, St. Petersburg, 1987. Art Gallery, Sydney, 1987.
Sezon Museum of Art, Tokyo, 1990. Musée de la Mode,
Marseille, 1993. Fondation Pierre Bergé–Yves Saint Laurent,
Paris, 2006.

84
Evening Ensemble
Fall–Winter 1976
Coat in lamé by Abraham. Jet embroidery
by Lesage. Mink trimming by Garande.
Passementerie by Leroux. Fur toque. Stone
and metal pendant earrings. Leather and
mink gloves. Leather boots.
Metropolitan Museum of Art, New York, 1983. Palace of
Fine Arts, Beijing, 1985. Musée des Arts de la Mode, Paris,
1986. Tretyakov Gallery, Moscow, 1986. State Hermitage
Museum, St. Petersburg, 1987. Musée de la Mode,
Marseille, 1993. Fondation Pierre Bergé–Yves Saint Laurent,
Paris, 2006.
Publications
Vogue, United States, December 1976.
Jours de France, France, December 1976.

85
Evening Ensemble
Fall–Winter 1976
Bolero in velvet by Gandini. Skirt of moiré by
Gandini. Velvet by Buche. Jet embroidery by
Lesage. Blouse in muslin by Bianchini. Turban
in satin by Abraham. Rhinestone, metal, and
jet pendant earrings. Metal and rhinestone
bracelets. Satin sandals with leather edging
and laces.
Metropolitan Museum of Art, New York, 1983. Palace of
Fine Arts, Beijing, 1985. Musée des Arts de la Mode, Paris,
1986. Tretyakov Gallery, Moscow, 1986. State Hermitage
Museum, St. Petersburg, 1987. Art Gallery, Sydney, 1987.
Sezon Museum of Art, Tokyo, 1990. Fondation Pierre Bergé–
Yves Saint Laurent, Paris, 2006.

86
Evening Ensemble
Fall–Winter 1969
Tunic and pants in silk lamé by Abraham.
Embroidery by Mesrine. Colored bead and
rhinestone earrings. Leather pumps.

87
Evening Suit
Fall–Winter 1981
Sequin, stone, and chenille embroidery by
Lesage. Pate de verre, metal, and plume
pendant earrings, rings, and bracelets.
Leather sandals.
Metropolitan Museum of Art, New York, 1983. Palace of
Fine Arts, Beijing, 1985. Musée des Arts de la Mode, Paris,
1986. Tretyakov Gallery, Moscow, 1986. State Hermitage
Museum, St. Petersburg, 1987. Art Gallery, Sydney, 1987.
Musée de la Mode, Marseille, 1993. Fondation Pierre Bergé–
Yves Saint Laurent, Paris, 2006.
Publication
Vogue, United States, January 1981.

88
Evening Gown
Fall–Winter 1986
Crushed velvet lamé by Abraham. Earrings
and necklace by Goossens. Cuffs by Roux.
Satin pumps.
Art Gallery, Sydney, 1987. Musée de la Mode, Marseille,
1993. Fondation Pierre Bergé–Yves Saint Laurent,
Paris, 2006.

89
Evening Gown
Fall–Winter 1991
Draped lamé. Metal bracelet. Leather and
rhinestone pumps.
Musée de la Mode, Marseille, 1993. Fondation Pierre Bergé–
Yves Saint Laurent, Paris, 2006.
Publication
Harper's Bazaar, Germany, December 1991.

COLORS AND TEXTURES

"RED IS THE BASIS FOR MAKE-UP, IT IS THE LIPS, THE NAILS. RED IS A NOBLE COLOR, A COLOR OF PRECIOUS STONES—THE RUBY— AND IT IS A DANGEROUS COLOR; SOMETIMES YOU HAVE TO PLAY WITH DANGER. RED IS RELIGIOUS, AND IT IS BLOOD, AND IT IS ROYAL, IT IS PHEDRA, AND A MULTITUDE OF HEROINES. RED LIGHT AND RED COMBAT, RED IS COMBAT BETWEEN LIFE AND DEATH."

Yves Saint Laurent (December 6, 1983), quoted by Laurence Benaïm, in *Yves Saint Laurent* (Paris: Grasset, 1993), p. 303.

The traditional rules of harmony of colors are reversed by new contrasts launched by the couturier. The tonalities of the hues clash and add dynamism to the brilliance of the clothing: turquoise-pink, green-orange, black-blue. The hues thus awakened use daring dissonances that revolutionize the sense of color in fashion. The couturier favors violence in the mixture of tones.

88 2784 X

Câllevn̈e/Sonia

Robe longue
prenessei en
crepe bleu
Turquoise de
Bucol 2701/796
et crepe marocain corail
Abrahan 3737/18
pour le haut
et le pan

1 collier ras le cou COURLANDE
cailloux de turquoise avec
quelques pierres rouges fermé
par deux coquilles - 2 Frangs -

B.O gossens - Créoles de
métal OR avec cœur
turquoise -

2 manchettes D. Roux métal
OR assymétriques.

escarpins
de satin
marron -

KM 19/1

95

96_1

7810

capuchon
de
tulle noir
Brodé
d'etoiles
oz

cape
rose vif
Brodé
oz
argent
diamant

Rayons

96_2

90
Full-Length Evening Gown
Spring–Summer 1969
Blouse in organza by Bucol. Skirt in
patchwork by Brossin de Méré. Belt in
satin ribbon by Guillemin. Leather sandals.
Made to order for Nan Kempner, Hélène
Rochas, and HRH The Duchess of Windsor.
Metropolitan Museum of Art, New York, 1983. Musée des
Arts de la Mode, Paris, 1986. Art Gallery, Sydney, 1987.
Fondation Pierre Bergé–Yves Saint Laurent, Paris, 2007.
Publication
Elle (cover), France, May 5, 1969.

91
Evening Ensemble
Spring–Summer 1970
Crêpe dress and coat. Passementerie, metal,
and bead necklace. Leather pumps.
Made to order for Nan Kempner.
Fondation Pierre Bergé–Yves Saint Laurent, Paris, 2007.

92
Evening Gown
Spring–Summer 1987
Crêpe by Abraham and Bucol. Plastic and
metal earrings by Goossens. Plastic and stone
choker by Courlande. Metal cuffs by Roux.
Satin pumps.
Art Gallery, Sydney, 1987.

93
Daytime Ensemble
Fall–Winter 1989
Woolen overcoat by Garigue with Trégal.
Blouse of crêpe by Taroni. Skirt in woolen
jersey by Racine. Belt in calf velour. Velvet
and felt hat. Wooden pendant earrings.
Leather gloves. Brocade boots.
Made to order for Sao Schlumberger.

94
Cocktail Ensemble
Spring–Summer 1989
Jacket in lamé brocade by Abraham. Blouse
and pant in crêpe by Abraham. Muslin belt
by Saris. Ceramic and paste gem pendant
earrings by Baschet. Rhinestone pins by
Sabbagh. Satin pumps.

95
Evening Ensemble
Fall–Winter 1992
Great-coat, dress, and belt in satin by
Abraham. Faceted glass cabochon pendant
earrings. Rocaille pendant by Leroux. Faille
and rhinestone sandals.
Musée de la Mode, Marseille, 1993.

96_1, 96_2
Evening Ensemble
Fall–Winter 2000
Cape in satin by Buche. Tulle by Sophie.
"Star" pattern sequin embroidery with
rocaille and metal thread by Lesage. Vest in
satin and velvet by Gandini. Skirt of crêpe by
Taroni. Stone and metal earrings. Lace and
sequin pumps.

97
Evening Ensemble
Spring–Summer 2002
Cape in silk gazar by Abraham. Lined
with taffeta by Buche. Dress in muslin by
Bianchini. Rhinestone and metal pendant
earrings and ring by Goossens. Satin sandals.

GEOMETRY

"HOW I ADAPTED RIGID LINES ON A BODY OF A WOMAN WHO MOVES, I CANNOT SAY."

Yves Saint Laurent

In black-and-white or in color, in diamonds, triangles, squares, lines, spots, and planes, pattern extends the possibilities of prints and embroidery. Geometry animates the surfaces of dresses and shirts into a vibrant optical pattern. The use of spots in different sizes in the 1992 summer collection changed the proportions of each part of the whole, which was formed by this total look.

5122
Blanche
Amanda

82

Abaham
44.329/74

55

100

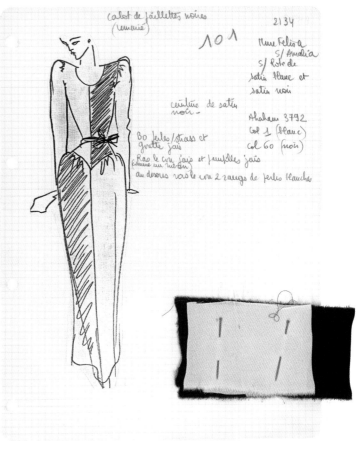

Calot de paillettes noires
(remonté)

101

2134

Mme Felisa
S/ Amalia
S/ Robe de
satin blanc et
satin noir

ceinture de satin
noir –

Abaham 3792
Col 1 (blanc)
Col 60 (noir)

Bo perles/strass et
gratte jais
Ras le cou jais et pampilles jais
couture au milieu
au dessous ras le cou 2 rangs de perles blanches

101

"I LOVE GOLD, A MAGICAL COLOR, FOR THE REFLECTION OF A WOMAN. IT IS THE COLOR OF THE SUN. I LOVE RED, AGGRESSIVE AND SAVAGE. THE FAWN COLORS OF THE DESERT. BUT FOR ME, BLACK IS A REFUGE BECAUSE IT EXPRESSES WHAT I WANT. WITH IT, EVERYTHING BECOMES SIMPLER, MORE LINEAR, MORE DRAMATIC."

Yves Saint Laurent, quoted by Laurence Benaïm, in *Yves Saint Laurent,* op. cit., p. 472.

98
Evening Gown
Fall–Winter 1968
Woolen fabric by Abraham. Passementerie
belt. Colored bead and metal stud earrings.
Leather pumps.
Made to order for Nan Kempner.
Fondation Pierre Bergé–Yves Saint Laurent, Paris, 2007.

99
"Op Art" Suit
Spring–Summer 1966
Jacket and skirt in herringbone wool by
Lesur. Leather belt and gloves. Patent leather
pumps with metal buckles designed by Yves
Saint Laurent and produced by Roger Vivier.
Made to order for Leslie Caron.
Publications
Vogue, United States, March 1, 1966.
Elle, France, March 10, 1966.

100
Cocktail Dress
Spring–Summer 1969
Crêpe by Abraham. Colored bead and
enamel stud earrings. Patent leather sandals.
Made to order for Nan Kempner.
Fondation Pierre Bergé–Yves Saint Laurent, Paris, 2007.
Publication
Epoca, Italy, February 2, 1969.

101
Evening Gown
Fall–Winter 1979
Satin crêpe by Abraham. Colored bead,
jet, and rhinestone pendant earrings.
Passementerie and jet bead choker. Chain of
colored beads and satin bow. Satin sandals.
Made to order for Nan Kempner.
Metropolitan Museum of Art, New York, 1983. Palace of
Fine Arts, Beijing, 1985. Fondation Pierre Bergé–Yves Saint
Laurent, Paris, 2007.
Publication
Vogue, France, September 1979.

102
Evening Ensemble
Fall–Winter 1984, no. 147
Domino in faille by Taroni. Bustier in organza
by Bianchini. Embroidery by Brossin de Méré.
Skirt in satin by Abraham. Passementerie
belt on moiré by Taroni. Metal, rhinestone,
and cabochon pendant earrings, with colored
beads by Sabbagh. Metal, rhinestone, and
crystal bracelet. Leather and tulle gloves.
Sandals with rhinestone buttons.
Palace of Fine Arts, Beijing, 1985. Musée des Arts de la
Mode, Paris, 1986. Tretyakov Gallery, Moscow, 1986. State
Hermitage Museum, St. Petersburg, 1987. Art Gallery,
Sydney, 1987. Sezon Museum of Art, Tokyo, 1990.
Publications
Vogue, Italy, September 1, 1984.
Harper's Bazaar, United States, September 1, 1984.

103
Cocktail Dress
Spring–Summer 1992
Silk gazar by Abraham. Straw picture hat
embroidered with sequins. Ceramic pendant
earrings by Baschet. Crêpe pumps.
Publication
Joyce, France, March 1992.

LYRICAL
SOURCES

Visionary and creator playing with colors, shapes, and materials, Yves Saint Laurent constantly renews his vision while respecting the principles of European classical elegance. The magnificently dressed Yves Saint Laurent woman never gives way to the option of disguise. But the Saint Laurent style also delves into the roots in its use of the spectacular and a certain theatricality. This sense of the sumptuous explodes in a multitude of themes nourished by artistic and literary curiosity and a vast culture. The creative impetus freely flourishes in the expression of its lyrical sources.

OVER TIME

"NOSTALGIA IS LIKE DREAMING AWAKE. I AM DEFINITIVELY A DREAMER."

Yves Saint Laurent

Historical references resist facile decoding because they are never literal quotations. The gilding of baroque furniture is transposed into clothing, while incorporating the etiquette of appearance and decorative art of the seventeenth and eighteenth centuries. The black velvet dress of 1980 evokes an imaginary period between the Middle Ages and the Renaissance, that never knew the corset or the farthingale. The 1997 winter collection was more explicitly inspired by the Court of the Valois dynasty, but there were no ruffs or busks for a remodeled Queen Catherine in supple black sheath dresses.

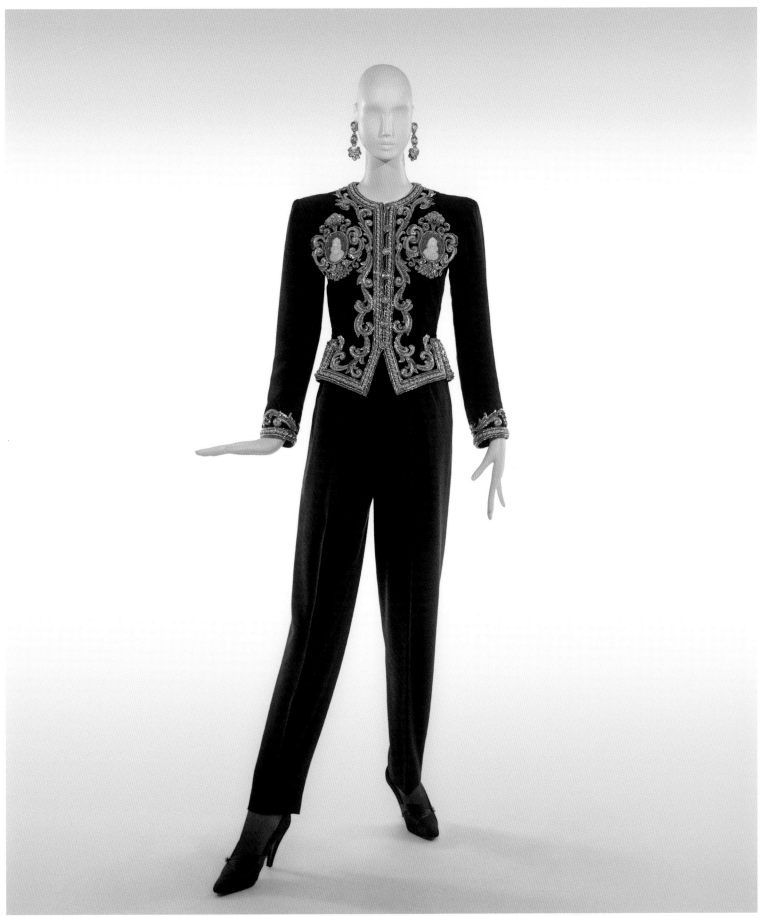

105

calligraphie –
Renée
Jacqueline

7168
Colette

104
Evening Gown
Fall–Winter 1980
Velvet by Buche. Patterned satin by
Abraham. Passementerie belt by Leroux.
Tulle veil. Passementerie and cabochon
wreath. Metal and stone necklace and cuffs.
Black velvet pumps.

105
Evening Ensemble
Fall–Winter 1984
Jacket in velvet by Moreau. "Cameo"
rocaille, bugle beads, and metal thread
embroidery by Lesage. Barathea pants by
Dormeuil. Metal and cabochon pendant
earrings. Cuffs by Goossens. Plume, metal,
and stone headdress. Draped crêpe pumps
with rhinestone buttons.
Musée des Arts de la Mode, Paris, 1986.

106
Evening Gown
Fall–Winter 1990
Figured moiré by Abraham. "Arabesque"
crystal embroidery by Lesage. Metal,
rhinestone, and crystal pendant earrings.
Satin sandals.

107
Evening Gown
Fall–Winter 1997
Velvet by Buche. Satin by Clerici. Metal,
diamond, and colored bead pendant earrings
by Baschet. Pate de verre, metal, and
rhinestone ring. Velvet pumps.

108
Evening Gown "Holbein"
Fall–Winter 1997
Silk satin by Clerici. Velvet by Buche. Stone
embroidery by Lesage. Metal, bead, and
stone pendant earrings. Suede and nutria
gloves by Lavabre Cadet. Velvet pumps.
Publication
Elle, United States, October 1, 1997.

DIALOGUE WITH ART

"MONDRIAN IS PURITY AND ONE CAN GO NO
FURTHER IN PURITY IN PAINTING. THIS IS A PURITY
THAT JOINS WITH THAT OF THE BAUHAUS. THE
MASTERPIECE OF THE TWENTIETH CENTURY IS
A MONDRIAN."

Yves Saint Laurent, quoted by Laurence Benaïm, in *Yves Saint Laurent* (Paris: Grasset, 1993), pp. 299–300.

Yves Saint Laurent and the Fondation Pierre Bergé–Yves Saint Laurent maintain important collections of works of art of all periods. In his childhood, Yves Saint Laurent painted, and paintings remain naturally at his side, just beneath the surface, when he creates his collections.

The couturier has paid homage to the work of artists whom he has admired, transposing the pictorial material into textiles. Some of his models continue a research into light as in the Impressionist tradition. Others rediscover the purity of the paintings of Piet Mondrian or Serge Poliakoff by cleverly inlaying the designs in jersey wool. The *Pop Art* collection, with its borrowings from Wesselman, breaks down the barriers between art and fashion in the spirit of Andy Warhol. From the sources of cubism, the creations salute the revolutionary work of Pablo Picasso and Georges Braque. The complex applications of fabric interpret, in a textile variation, Matisse's paper cut-outs. Even the subjects of the paintings come to life in the movement of the embroidered garments in homage to Vincent van Gogh and Auguste Renoir.

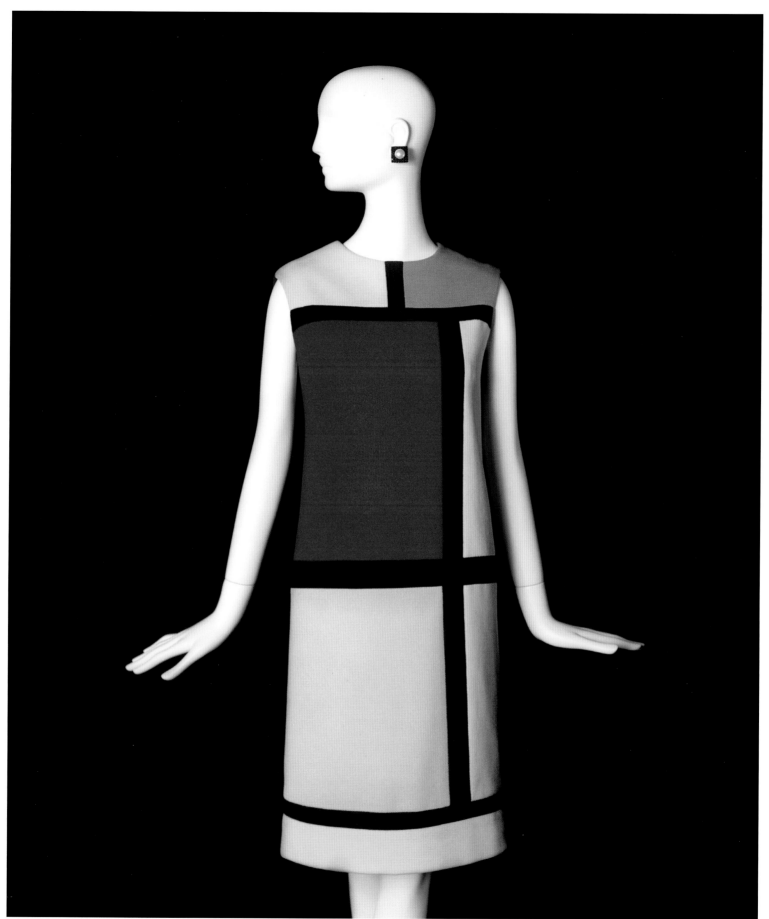

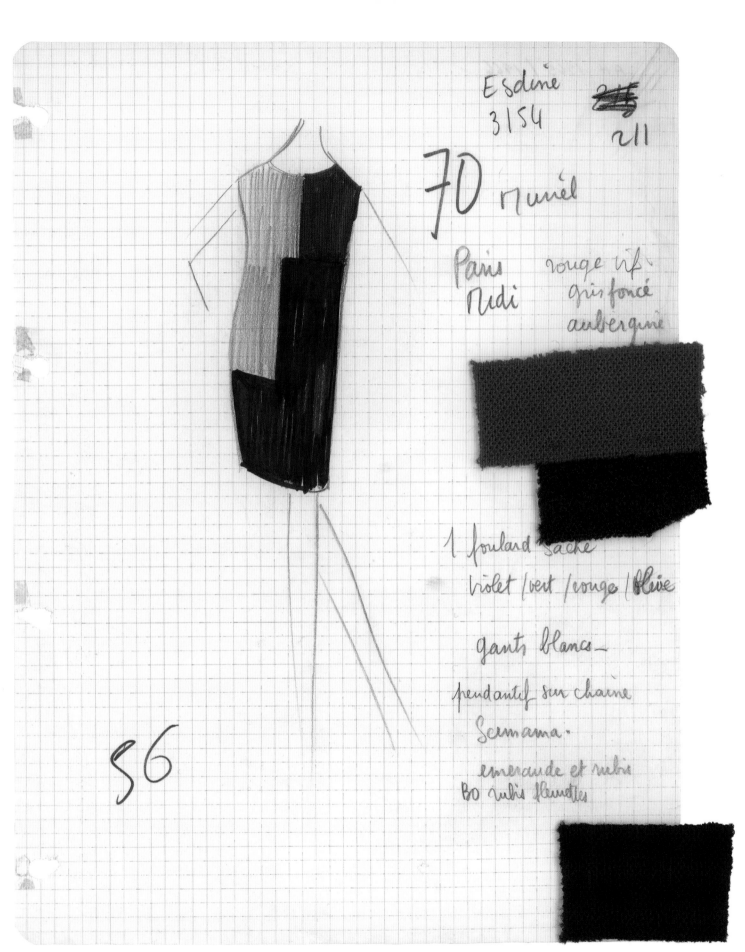

Esdine
3154   211

70 muriel

Paris   rouge vif
Midi   gris foncé
               aubergine

1 foulard sache
violet / vert / rouge / olive

gants blancs —

pendantif sur chaine
Scemama.

emeraude et rubis
Bo rubis flanelles

S6

111

112

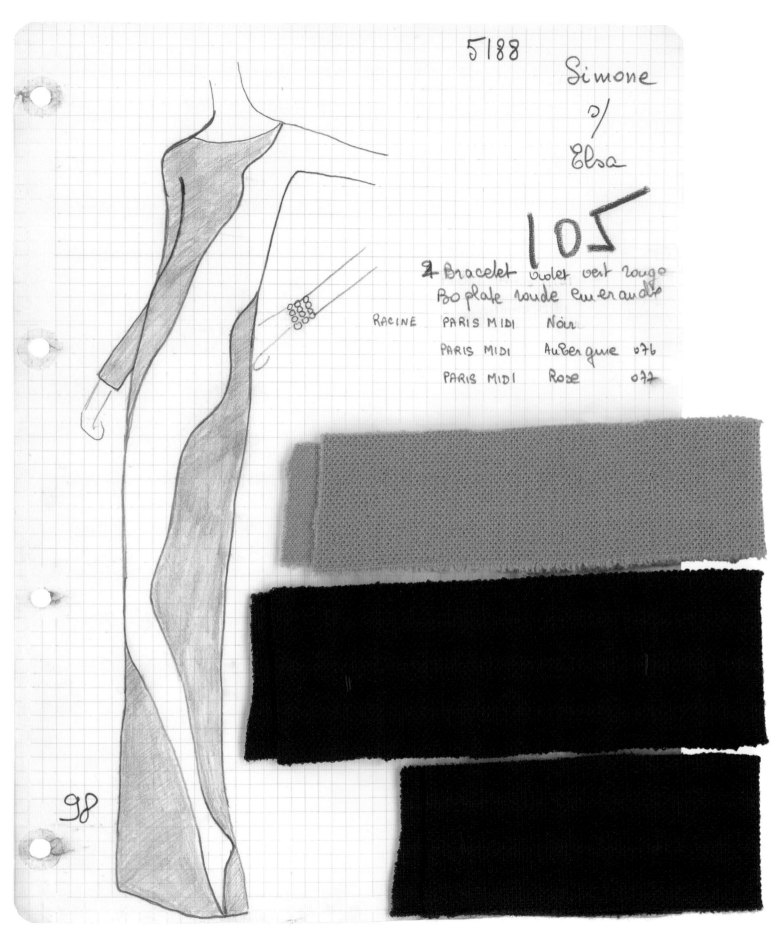

5188

Simone
s/
Elsa

105

1 Bracelet violet vert rouge
Bo plate ronde emeraude

RACINE	PARIS MIDI	Noir	
	PARIS MIDI	Aubergine	076
	PARIS MIDI	Rose	072

98

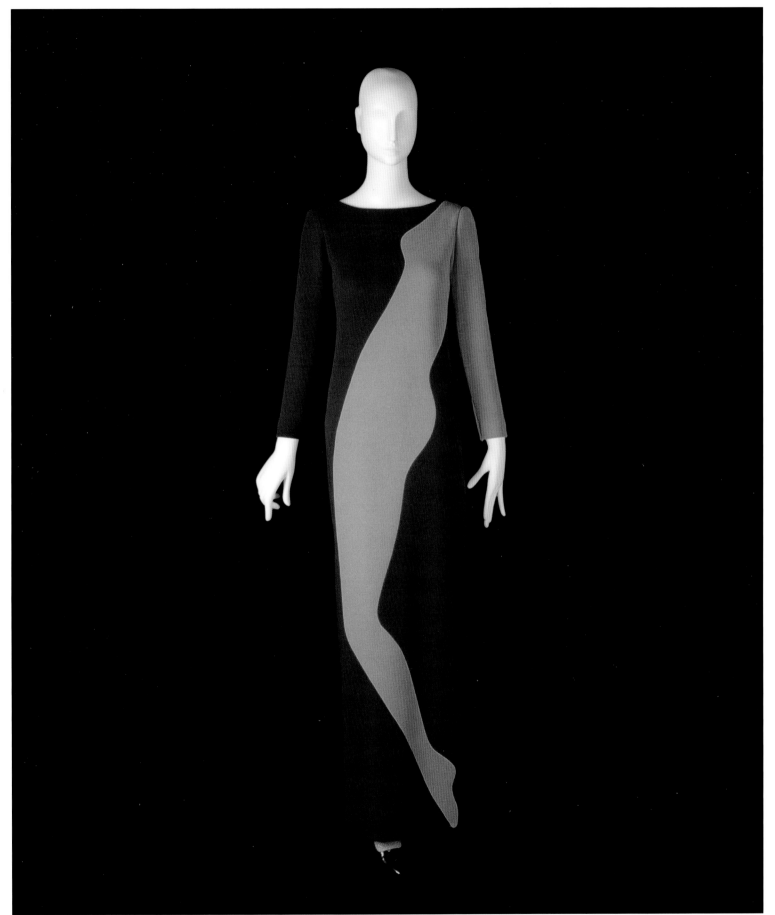

113_2

"PICASSO IS THE GENIUS OF THE PURE STATE. HE IS BURSTING WITH LIFE AND OPENNESS. PICASSO DOES NOT HAVE PURITY. HE IS THE BAROQUE. HE RUNS SEVERAL RACES, SHOOTS WITH SEVERAL BOWS, SEVERAL ARROWS TO HIS BOW."

Yves Saint Laurent, quoted by Laurence Benaïm, in *Yves Saint Laurent,* op. cit., p. 301.

115_1

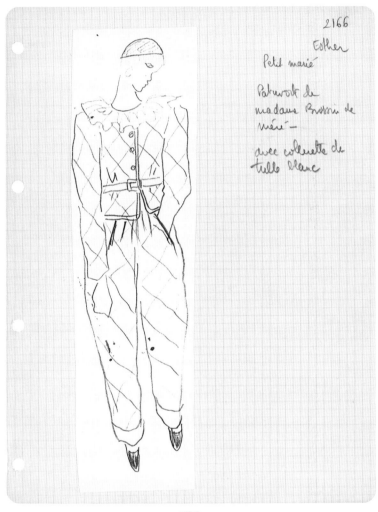

2166

Esther

Petit marié

Patrwork de
madame Brossin de
mère —

avec collerette de
tulle blanc

Marquis –
Dennes
5 B/S 38457/28/ais

collerettes de tulle noir
(col et poignets)

2165.

Esther.

Bouquet de
roses à la
main

Robe de mariée

en patchwork
pastel gris/bleu/jaune/rose
de madame Brossin
de Mère —

cocarde en satin
rose sur la queue
de cheval.

B·O perles pendantes
et strass

115_2

115_3

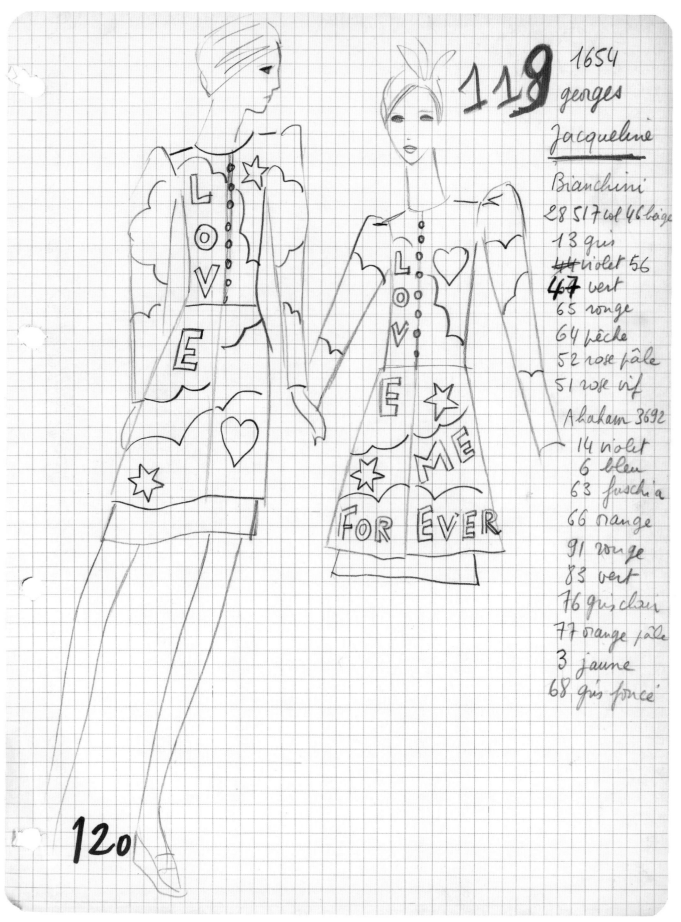

LOVE E ♥ ✦

LOVE ♥
E ✦ ME
✦ FOR EVER

118 1654
georges
Jacqueline

Bianchini
28 517 col 46 beige
13 gris
~~44~~ violet 56
47 vert
65 rouge
64 pêche
52 rose pâle
51 rose vif

Abraham 3692
14 violet
6 bleu
63 fuschia
66 orange
91 rouge
83 vert
76 gris clair
77 orange pâle
3 jaune
68 gris foncé

120

Le Marchand
14 Rs 1638/14
Jais

123   2098 X

Mme Felisa
s/ Kinet

Robe de taffetas
bleu et blanc

Bûche 103 col blanc
Tauri 3057 col 817
Bleu

Jupon de taffetas
bleu

Ceinture Noeud de
velours NOIR -

B.O Céramique noire
rocaille Bleu noir,
pierre irisée Bleue et
rubis.

125

4013
jungs

Double
Rose

126_1

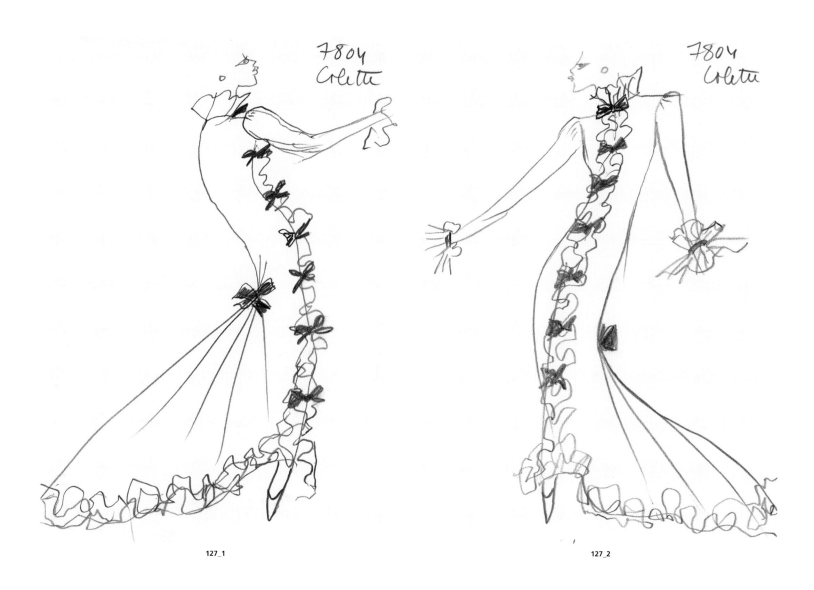

127_1

127_2

109
Cocktail Dress in Tribute to Piet Mondrian
Fall–Winter 1965
Jersey wool insets by Racine Paris Midi. Faceted jet and colored bead stud earrings. Patent leather pumps with metal buckles designed by Yves Saint Laurent and produced by Roger Vivier.

Metropolitan Museum of Art, New York, 1983. Palace of Fine Arts, Beijing, 1985. Musée des Arts de la Mode, Paris, 1986. Tretyakov Gallery, Moscow, 1986. State Hermitage Museum, St. Petersburg, 1987. Art Gallery, Sydney, 1987. Sezon Museum of Art, Tokyo, 1990. Musée de la Mode, Marseille, 1993. Fondation Pierre Bergé–Yves Saint Laurent, Paris 2004.

Publications

Vogue (cover), France, September 1965.

Vogue, United States, September 1965.

Harper's Bazaar, United States, September 1965.

The Connoisseur (cover), United States, February 1990.

110
Cocktail Dress in Tribute to Serge Poliakoff
Fall–Winter 1965
Jersey wool insets by Racine Paris Midi. Passementerie and faceted jet stud earrings. Patent leather pumps with metal buckles designed by Yves Saint Laurent and produced by Roger Vivier.

Metropolitan Museum of Art, New York, 1983. Art Gallery, Sydney, 1987. Sezon Museum of Art, Tokyo, 1990.

111
Cocktail Dress in Tribute to Piet Mondrian
Fall–Winter 1965
Insets in woolen jersey by Racine Paris Midi. Faceted jet and colored bead stud earrings. Patent leather pumps with metal buckles created by Yves Saint Laurent and produced by Roger Vivier.

Metropolitan Museum of Art, New York, 1983. Palace of Fine Arts, Beijing, 1985. Musée des Arts de la Mode, Paris, 1986. Tretyakov Gallery, Moscow, 1986. State Hermitage Museum, St. Petersburg, 1987. Art Gallery, Sydney, 1987. Fondation Pierre Bergé–Yves Saint Laurent, Paris, 2004.

Publications

Femme Chic, France, January 1965.

Elle (cover), France, January 27, 1992.

112
Cocktail Dress in Tribute to Tom Wesselmann
Fall–Winter 1966
Woolen jersey Racine Paris Midi. Encrusted "face." Faceted jet and colored bead stud earrings. Lamé pantyhose. Patent leather pumps.

Metropolitan Museum of Art, New York, 1983. Palace of Fine Arts, Beijing, 1985. Musée des Arts de la Mode, Paris, 1986. Tretyakov Gallery, Moscow, 1986. State Hermitage Museum, St. Petersburg, 1987. Art Gallery, Sydney, 1987. Sezon Museum of Art, Tokyo, 1990. Fondation Pierre Bergé–Yves Saint Laurent, Paris, 2004.

Publications

Life, United States, October 1966.

Vogue, France, December 1983.

113_1, 113_2
Full-Length Evening Gown in Tribute to Tom Wesselmann
Fall–Winter, 1966
Woolen jersey by Racine Paris Midi. Encrusted "body." Lamé pantyhose. Patent leather pumps.

Metropolitan Museum of Art, New York, 1983. Palace of Fine Arts, Beijing, 1985. Musée des Arts de la Mode, Paris, 1986. Tretyakov Gallery, Moscow, 1986. State Hermitage Museum, St. Petersburg, 1987. Art Gallery, Sydney, 1987. Sezon Museum of Art, Tokyo, 1990. Fondation Pierre Bergé–Yves Saint Laurent, Paris, 2004.

Publications

Life (cover), United States, September 1966.

New York, United States, November 28, 1983.

114
Cocktail Dress in Tribute to Pablo Picasso
Fall–Winter 1979
Satin by Carlatto. Velvet by Léonard. "Face" embroidery of sequins, bugle beads, and rocaille by Lesage. Sequined velvet leaf turban. Metal and rhinestone pendant earrings. Metal, pearl, and rhinestone bracelets. Satin sandals with grosgrain and tulle "point d'esprit" bows.

Metropolitan Museum of Art, New York, 1983. Palace of Fine Arts, Beijing, 1985. Musée des Arts de la Mode, Paris, 1986. Tretyakov Gallery, Moscow, 1986. State Hermitage Museum, St. Petersburg, 1987. Art Gallery, Sydney, 1987. Sezon Museum of Art, Tokyo, 1990. Fondation Pierre Bergé–Yves Saint Laurent, Paris, 2004.

Publication

Vogue, France, September 1979.

115_1, 115_2, 115_3
Evening Ensembles in Tribute to Pablo Picasso
Fall–Winter 1979
Blouse and belt of "point d'esprit" tulle by Hurel. "Harlequin" skirt in satin patchwork, faille, and velvet by Brossin de Méré. Enamel and rhinestone stud earrings. Satin belt. Satin pumps. Boy (_2): "Harlequin" jacket and pants in taffeta patchwork by Brossin de Méré. Tulle trimmings. Velvet hat. Patent leather shoes. Girl (_3): "Harlequin" dress in taffeta patchwork by Brossin de Méré. Tulle trimmings. Velvet and feather hat. Rhinestone, colored bead, and metal pendant earrings. Patent leather shoes.

Metropolitan Museum of Art, New York, 1983. Palace of Fine Arts, Beijing, 1985. Musée des Arts de la Mode, Paris, 1986. Tretyakov Gallery, Moscow, 1986. State Hermitage Museum, St. Petersburg, 1987. Art Gallery, Sydney, 1987.

116
Evening Gown
Fall–Winter 1969
Crêpe georgette by Abraham. Stole in crêpe georgette by Abraham. "Bust" sculpture in galvanized copper created by Claude Lalanne.

Metropolitan Museum of Art, New York, 1983. Musée des Arts de la Mode, Paris, 1986. Tretyakov Gallery, Moscow, 1986. State Hermitage Museum, St. Petersburg, 1987. Art Gallery, Sydney, 1987. Sezon Museum of Art, Tokyo, 1990. Musée de la Mode, Marseille, 1993. Fondation Pierre Bergé–Yves Saint Laurent, Paris, 2004.

Publications

Paris Match, France, August 23, 1969.

Vogue, France, December 1983.

Elle, United Kingdom, April 2002.

117
Evening Gown
Fall–Winter 1969
Crêpe georgette by Abraham. Stole in crêpe georgette by Abraham. "Waist" sculpture in galvanized copper created by Claude Lalanne.

Metropolitan Museum of Art, New York, 1983. Musée des Arts de la Mode, Paris, 1986. Tretyakov Gallery, Moscow, 1986. State Hermitage Museum, St. Petersburg, 1987. Art Gallery, Sydney, 1987. Sezon Museum of Art, Tokyo, 1990. Musée de la Mode, Marseille, 1993. Fondation Pierre Bergé–Yves Saint Laurent, Paris, 2004.

Publications

Paris Match, France, August 23, 1969.

Elle, France, January 27, 1992.

Elle, United Kingdom, April 2002.

118
Bridal Gown
Fall–Winter 1970
Coat and skirt in velvet by Bianchini. Embroidered incrustations on satin. Draped velvet turban. Leather gloves. Satin platform sandals.

Metropolitan Museum of Art, New York, 1983. Palace of Fine Arts, Beijing, 1985.

119
Evening Gown in Tribute to Henri Matisse
Fall–Winter 1980
Top of velvet by Moreau. Moiré faille by Taroni. Satin appliqué "leaf" embroidery. Taffeta. Silk gazar. Velvet and faille by Brossin de Méré. Satin belt by Brossin de Méré. Plastic and rhinestone pendant earrings and necklace. Cabochon and metal bracelets. Satin sandals with bows.

Musée des Arts de la Mode, Paris, 1986. Tretyakov Gallery, Moscow, 1986. State Hermitage Museum, St. Petersburg, 1987. Art Gallery, Sydney, 1987. Sezon Museum of Art, Tokyo, 1990. Fondation Pierre Bergé–Yves Saint Laurent, Paris, 2004.

Publication

Vogue, France, September 1980.

120
Evening Gown in Homage to Henri Matisse
Fall–Winter 1981
Taffeta by Taroni and Buche. Taffeta flying panels by Lemarié. Velvet belt by Buche. Ceramic, pearl, stone, and glass stud earrings. Oversewn suede pumps.

Metropolitan Museum of Art, New York, 1983. Palace of Fine Arts, Beijing, 1985. Musée des Arts de la Mode, Paris, 1986. Tretyakov Gallery, Moscow, 1986. State Hermitage Museum, St. Petersburg, 1987. Fondation Pierre Bergé–Yves Saint Laurent, Paris, 2004.

Publication

Vogue, France, December 1983.

121
Evening Ensemble in Tribute to Henri Matisse
Fall–Winter 1981
Romanian blouse in fine wool by Dormeuil. Sequin, bugle bead, rocaille, silk, and chenille embroidery by Lesage. Skirt in velvet by Dormeuil. Moleskin fez. Velvet belt. Jet and trimmings by Leroux. Velvet pumps.

Musée des Arts de la Mode, Paris, 1986. Tretyakov Gallery, Moscow, 1986. State Hermitage Museum, St. Petersburg, 1987. Art Gallery, Sydney, 1987. Sezon Museum of Art, Tokyo, 1990. Fondation Pierre Bergé–Yves Saint Laurent, Paris, 2004.

Publication

Vogue, United States, January 1981.

122
Irises **Ensemble in Tribute to Vincent Van Gogh**
Spring–Summer 1988
Jacket, sequin, bugle bead, rocaille, and ribbon embroidery by Lesage. Silk crêpe skirt. Ceramic stud earrings. Satin gloves. Straw and silk hat. Faille pumps.

Sezon Museum of Art, Tokyo, 1990. Musée de la Mode, Marseille, 1993. Fondation Pierre Bergé–Yves Saint Laurent, Paris, 2004.

Publications

L'Officiel, France, March 1988.

Elle, France, January 27, 1992.

123
Sunflowers **Ensemble in Tribute to Vincent Van Gogh**
Spring–Summer 1988
Jacket, sequin, bugle bead, rocaille, and ribbon embroidery by Lesage. Silk crêpe skirt. Ceramic stud earrings. Satin gloves. Straw and silk hat. Crepe pumps.

Sezon Museum of Art, Tokyo, 1990. Musée de la Mode, Marseille, 1993. Fondation Pierre Bergé–Yves Saint Laurent, Paris, 2004.

Publications

L'Officiel, France, March 1988.

124
Evening Gown in Tribute to Georges Braque
Spring–Summer 1988
Silk crêpe by Gandini. "Dove" embroidery in sequins and rocaille by Lesage. "Dove" rhinestone, metal earrings and rock crystal, metal bracelet by Goossens. Satin pumps.

Fondation Pierre Bergé–Yves Saint Laurent, Paris, 2004.

Publications

Paris Match, France, February 12, 1988.

Vogue, United States, April 1988.

125
Evening Gown in Tribute to Georges Braque
Spring–Summer 1988
Silk satin by Gandini. "Doves and guitar" embroidery of sequins, bugle beads, paillettes, rocaille, and suede by Lesage. Satin pumps.

Sezon Museum of Art, Tokyo, 1990. Fondation Pierre Bergé–Yves Saint Laurent, Paris, 2004.

Publications

Vogue, United States, April 1988.

Harper's Bazaar, Germany, May 1988.

126_1, 126_2
Evening Ensembles in Tribute to Georges Braque
Spring–Summer 1988
Cape in worsted (_1) and gazar (_2) by Garigue. "Face" embroidery in ottoman, sequins, and rocaille by Lesage. Robe, scarf, and belt in muslin by Bianchini and Saris. Metal and rhinestone necklace by Goossens. "Dove" metal and rhinestone earrings by Sabbagh. Faille pumps.

Fondation Pierre Bergé–Yves Saint Laurent, Paris, 2004.

Publications

Paris Match, France, February 12, 1988.

Tatler, United Kingdom, April 1988.

127_1, 127_2
Bridal Gown in Tribute to Auguste Renoir
Fall–Winter 2000
Moiré by Bucol. Flying panels in taffeta by Buche. Tulle by Hurel. "Point d'esprit" by Lemarié. Velvet ribbon bows. Metal and rhinestone pendant earrings by Baschet. Satin T-strap shoes with leather laces.

LITERATURE

"I HAVE PRODUCED A WHOLE COLLECTION IN HOMAGE TO SHAKESPEARE. A BLOUSE WILL EVOKE HAMLET'S SHIRT, A RED SILK DRESS THAT OF LADY MACBETH; IT WAS A REMINDER OF THE MIDDLE AGES, BUT ABSOLUTELY MODERN. SOMETIMES, I ALSO THINK ABOUT EMMA BOVARY. THIS CHARACTER IS EXTREMELY CONTEMPORARY. MADAME BOVARY EXPRESSES THE DISSATISFACTION OF WOMEN, WHICH IS THE SAME TODAY AS IT WAS A CENTURY AGO. I FIND VIVIEN LEIGH SUBLIME IN *A STREETCAR NAMED DESIRE*. HER FRAGILE PERSONALITY DRESSED IN A SUMPTUOUS CASTOFF FASCINATES ME."

Interview with Catherine Deneuve, *Globe*, France, May 1, 1986.

As a passionate reader of the masterpieces of classical literature, Yves Saint Laurent brings his heroes to life on the stage, such as Lady Macbeth or Oscar Wilde in the black velvet costume of an aesthete. Apollinaire, Louis Aragon, Elsa Triolet, and Jean Cocteau leave their words in embroidered writing with surrealist accents.

Felisa   3050

minori
St
mounia

128

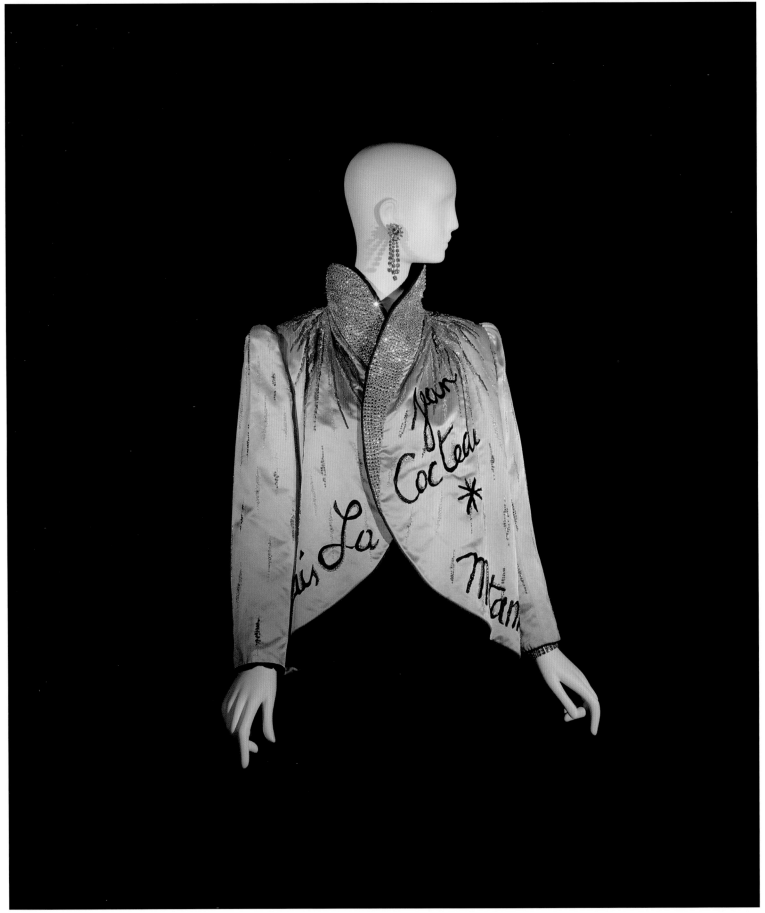

129_1

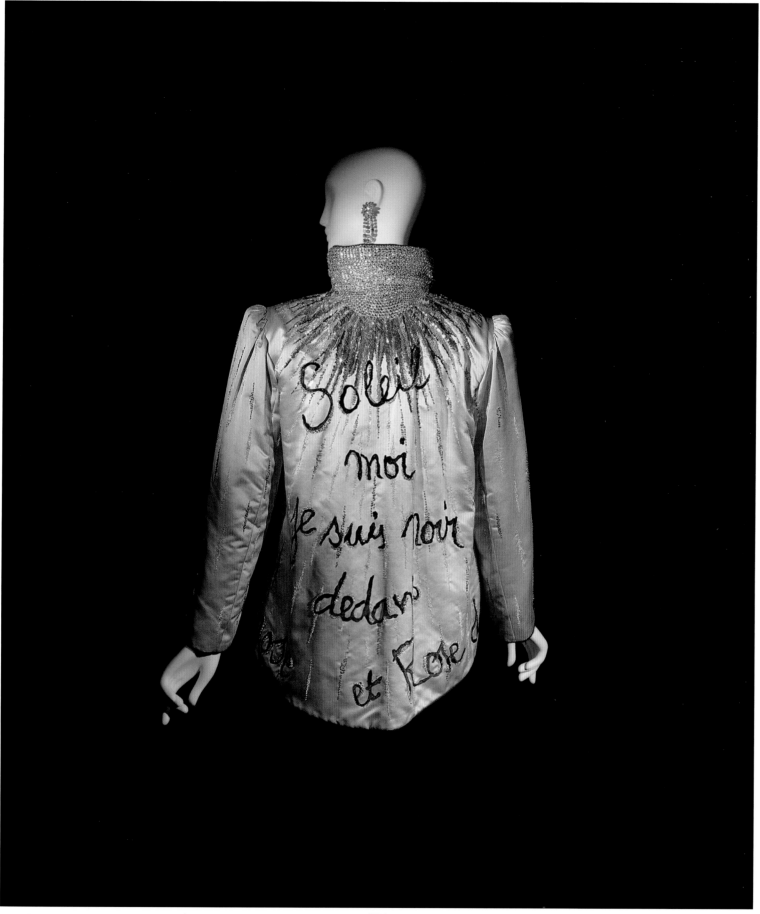

130

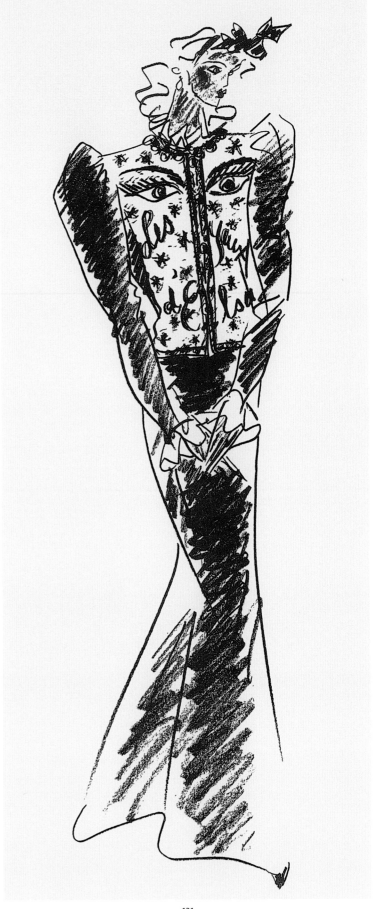

131

6 233
Jean Livre
veste
6 2 33 bis
Knichers

132

197

128
Evening Ensemble
Fall–Winter 1978
Jacket in velvet by Léonard. Rhinestone, metal thread, and plastic embroidery by Lesage. Velvet skirt by Léonard. Velvet and satin toque. Metal and rhinestone cabochon pendant earrings. Faille pumps.
Metropolitan Museum of Art, New York, 1983. Palace of Fine Arts, Beijing, 1985. Musée des Arts de la Mode, Paris, 1986. Tretyakov Gallery, Moscow, 1986. Art Gallery, Sydney, 1987. Sezon Museum of Art, Tokyo, 1990.

129_1, 129_2
Evening Ensemble in Tribute to Jean Cocteau
Fall–Winter 1980
Great-coat in satin by Léonard. Velvet by Moreau. Sequin, metal thread, and rhinestone embroidery by Lesage. Dress in velvet by Moreau. Metal and rhinestone pendant earrings and bracelets by Sabbagh. Pearl and metal necklace by Caillol. Colored bead chains. Satin pumps.
Metropolitan Museum of Art, New York, 1983. Palace of Fine Arts, Beijing, 1985. Tretyakov Gallery, Moscow, 1986. Musée des Arts de la Mode, Paris, 1986. Art Gallery, Sydney, 1987. Sezon Museum of Art, Tokyo, 1990. Musée de la Mode, Marseille, 1993.
Publications
Vogue, Italy, September 1980.
Jardin des modes, France, January 1984.
Elle, France, February, 15, 1988.

130
Evening Ensemble in Tribute to Guillaume Apollinaire
Fall–Winter 1980
Velvet by Moreau and Buche. Rhinestone embroidery by Lesage. Jet pompons by Leroux. Suede belt with rhinestone-covered buckles by Hamon. Metal and rhinestone pendant earrings by Sabbagh. Faceted jet, colored bead, and rhinestone chains and choker. Satin sandals with leather edging and laces.
Musée des Arts de la Mode, Paris, 1986. Art Gallery, Sydney, 1987. Sezon Museum of Art, Tokyo, 1990.
Publications
Vogue, Germany, January 1980.
Vogue, Italy, September 1980.

131
Evening Ensemble in Tribute to Louis Aragon
Fall–Winter 1980
Jacket in velvet by Moreau and Gandini. Sequin, bead, and metal thread embroidery by Lesage. Blouse in patterned silk by Abraham. Skirt in velvet by Buche. Metal, stone, rhinestone, and colored bead earrings and ring by Goossens. Satin sandals with bow and leather laces.
Metropolitan Museum of Art, New York, 1983. Palace of Fine Arts, Beijing, 1985. Musée des Arts de la Mode, Paris, 1986. Tretyakov Gallery, Moscow, 1986. Art Gallery, Sydney, 1987. Sezon Museum of Art, Tokyo, 1990.
Publication
L'Officiel, France, January 9, 1980.

132
Tuxedo in Tribute to Oscar Wilde
Fall–Winter 1993
Jacket and vest in velvet by Moreau. Piped trim in satin leather by Abraham. Blouse in satin by Taroni and Buche. Silk jersey breeches by Racine. Satin cravat. Rhinestone cabochon earrings by Boutron. "Heart" metal and rhinestone cuff buttons. Velvet strap sandals with satin laces.
Musée de la Mode, Marseille, 1993.

133
Bridal Gown in Tribute to William Shakespeare
Fall–Winter 1980
Damassé Abraham. Satin Taroni. Lamé Bucol and Bianchini. Ganse by Merieux. Crown and silver net veil. Sparkled fishnet, pearl, and rhinestone pendant earrings. Metal and paste gem cuffs and rings. Rhinestone cross choker. Rhinestone and jet pearl chains. Metal and pearl brooch. Silver brocade pumps.
Metropolitan Museum of Art, New York, 1983. Palace of Fine Arts, Beijing, 1985. Musée des Arts de la Mode, Paris, 1986. Tretyakov Gallery, Moscow, 1986. State Hermitage Museum, St. Petersburg, 1987.
Publications
Vogue, France, September 1980.
Vogue, France, December 1983.

GLAMOUR

"HAPPY MEMORIES, AS WELL, ALL THE COSTUMES AND SETS THAT I DESIGNED FOR THE THEATER AND THE OPERA. I WAS TORN BETWEEN THE THEATER AND FASHION. IT WAS MY MEETING WITH CHRISTIAN DIOR THAT GUIDED ME TOWARD FASHION."

Yves Saint Laurent, *Glamour,* France, May 1, 1994.

As a child Yves Saint Laurent believed he was destined for the stage. He had a revelation about it in Oran, in 1947, when he attended a performance of Molière's *School for Women,* directed by Louis Jouvet, with sets by Christian Bérard. He was obsessed with a single idea: to go to Paris to design theatrical costumes. Being hired by Christian Dior would change his destiny. But a love of spectacle remains very much alive in his collections. He loves the theatricalization of women seen in a modern light through Hollywood movies. He uses movie-star glamour to reinvent the aesthetic of the vamp.

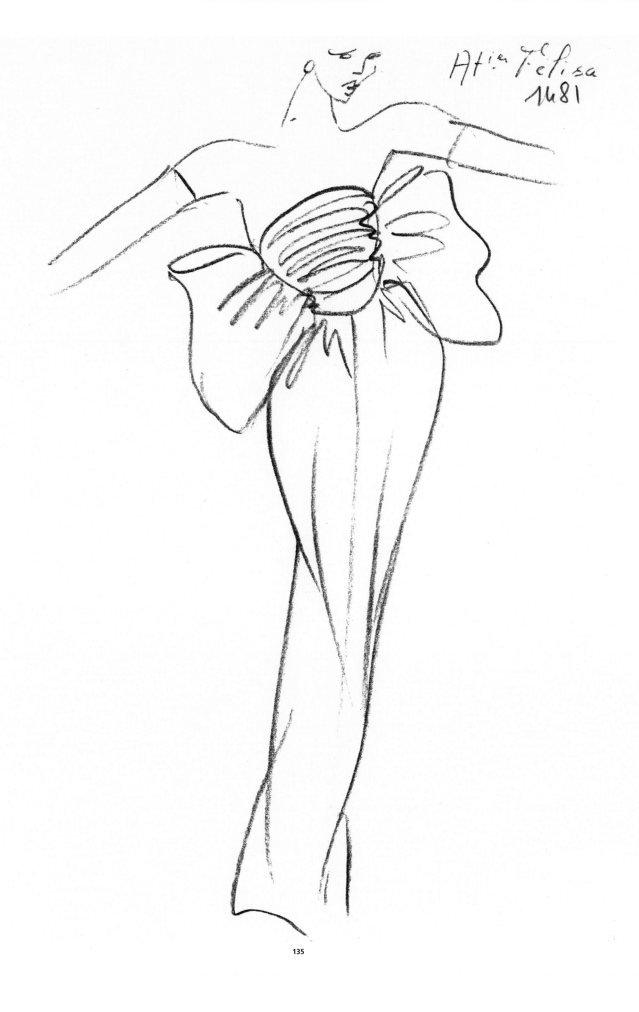

135

Dessus.
7 BS Nacre bl. Ø20
16 « « Ø16

Feutre d'homme blanc
écharpe de mousseline
blanche -

Pochette en crêpe de chine blanc

1118

Jean Pierre

S/ Anita

Ceinture
lézard blanc

13

Costume croisé en
gabardine blanche.

Dormeuil 981 286
col blanc

BO rondes jules et or

Fleur
7295

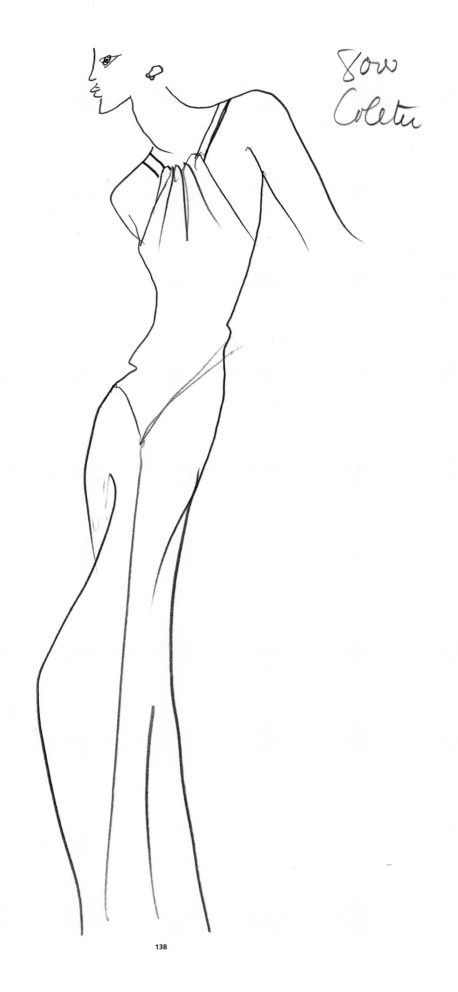

pour
Colette

Colette
8031
Alec

134
Evening Gown in Tribute to
Marilyn Monroe
Spring–Summer 1990
Sequined muslin by Schlaeffer. Embroidered
pompons by Lisbeth. Glass cabochon ring.
Silk satin pumps.
Made to order for Catherine Deneuve.
Publication
Harper's Bazaar, France, March 1990.

135
Evening Gown
Fall–Winter 1983
Bustier and duchesse satin bow by Abraham.
Skirt in velvet by Moreau. Faceted cabochon
and metal chocker. Metal and rhinestone
pendant earrings and cuffs. Silk crêpe
sandals.
Musée des Arts de la Mode, Paris, 1986. Tretyakov Gallery,
Moscow, 1986. State Hermitage Museum, St. Petersburg,
1987. Art Gallery, Sydney, 1987.
Publications
F.A.Z. (cover), Germany, November 28, 1986.
Harper's Bazaar, United States, March 1991.
Vogue, Spain, June 2001.

136
Pantsuit
Spring–Summer 1979
Jacket and pants in wool gabardine by
Dormeuil. Blouse in silk satin by Taroni. Metal
and colored bead stud earrings and cuff
buttons. Satin pumps.
Publications
L'Officiel, France, March 1, 1979.
Vogue, United States, April 1, 1979.

137
Evening Gown
Fall–Winter 1998
Silk crêpe by Gandini. Velvet ribbon by
Rodolphe Simon. Metal and colored bead
pendant earrings by Baschet. Glass cabochon
ring. Silk satin sandals with rhinestone
buckles.

138
Evening Ensemble
Spring–Summer 2001
Coat in gauze by Bianchini. Trim with
ostrich feathers by Lemarié. Dress in crêpe
satin by Buche. Metal and rhinestone
pendant earrings. Silk crêpe sandals.
Publications
Vogue, United Kingdom, April 2001.
Vogue, Spain, April 2001.

139
Full-Length Evening Gown
Spring–Summer 2001
Tulle by Rodolphe Simon. Satin ribbon by
Guillemin. Organza flower by Lemarié.
Colored bead and metal pendant earrings.
Leather sandals.
Publications
Elle, France, February 2001.
Vogue, Spain, April 2001.
Elle, France, May 2001.

ANIMALS

"FEATHER AND MUSLIN ARE LIKE A CARESS."
Yves Saint Laurent

The opulence of materials translates into an original exoticism, far from postcard representations. The woman adorns herself in a trompe l'oeil masterpiece of plumes and furs. The exotic animal of haute couture ends up stuffed, but is tamed in muslin, crocodile leather, or printed, or embroidered evoking furs, the plumage of birds, or fish scales.

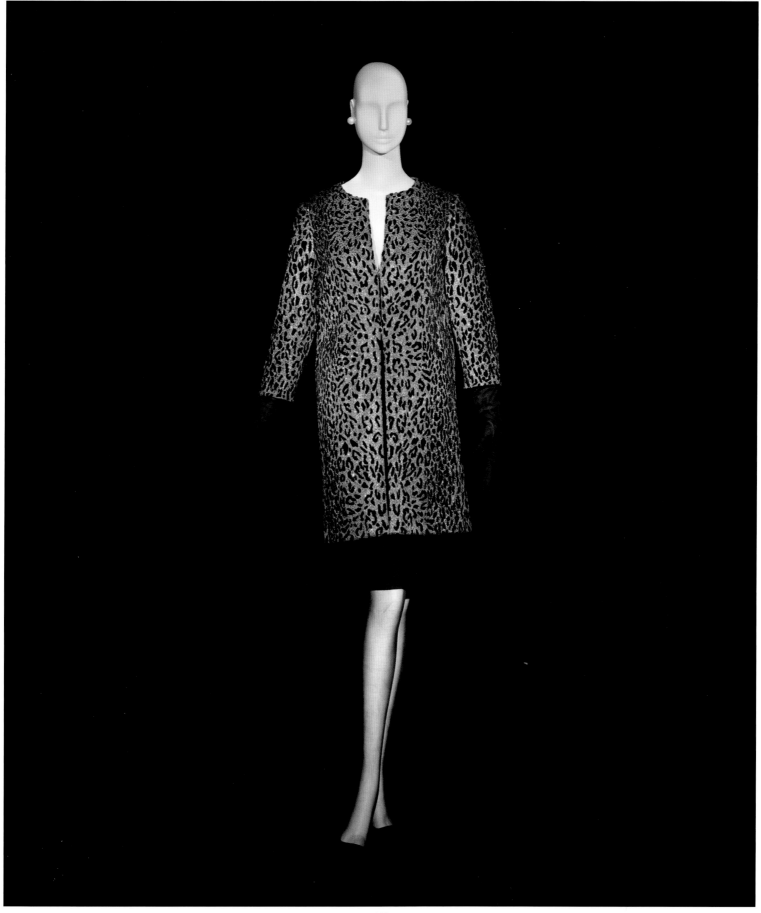

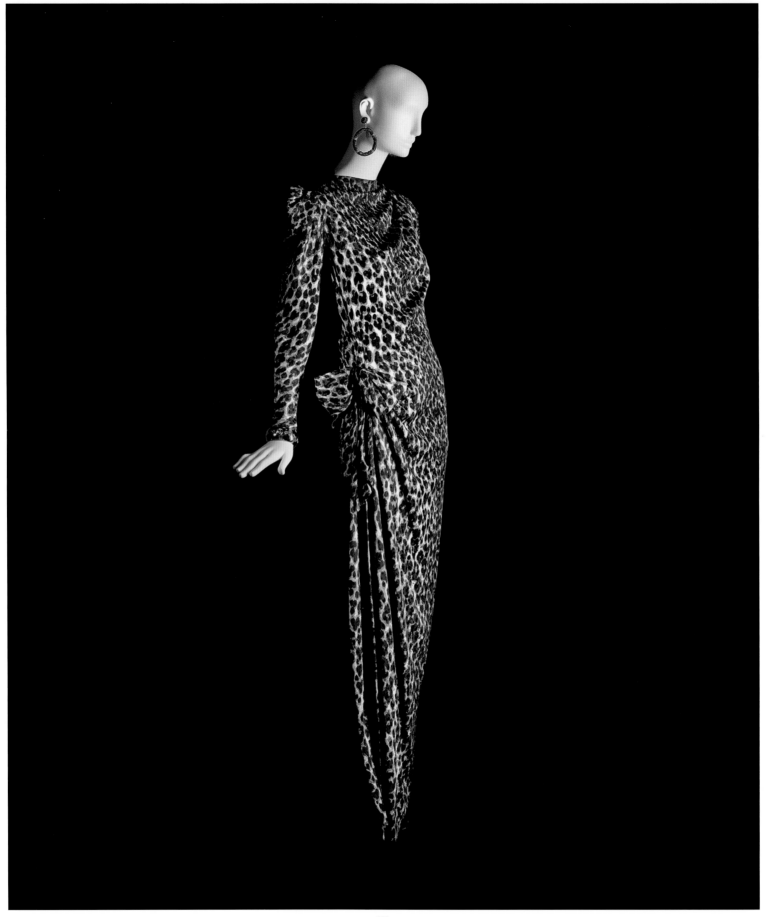

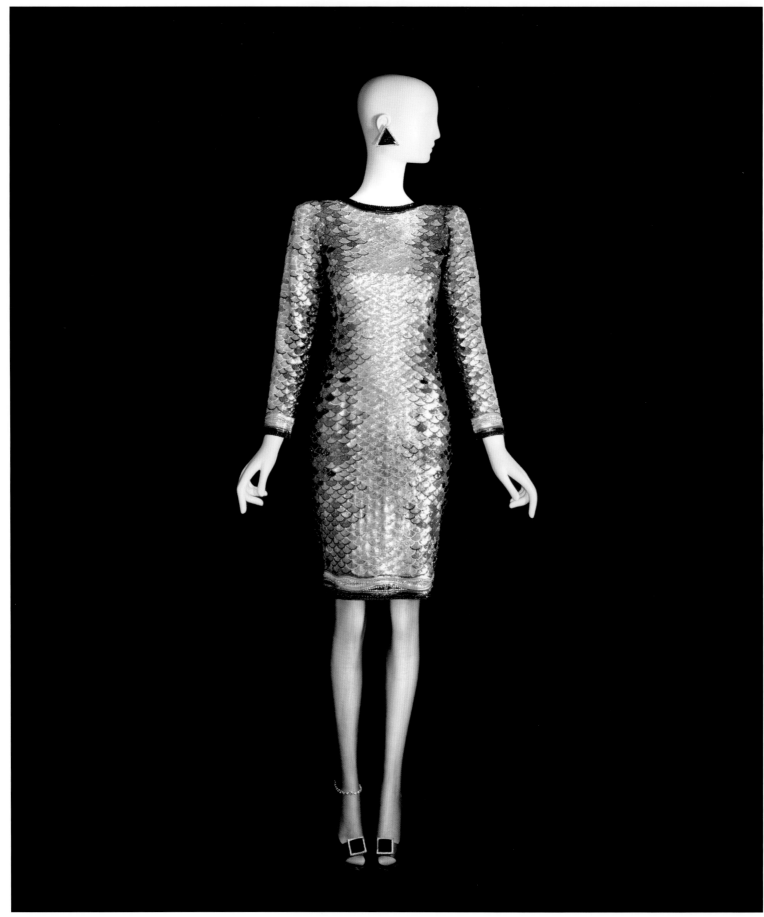

140
Evening Ensemble
Fall–Winter 1964
Coat, sequin, metal thread, and chenille embroidery by Rébé. Skirt in wool by Fournier. Colored bead stud earrings. Suede gloves and pumps.
Metropolitan Museum of Art, New York, 1983. Palace of Fine Arts, Beijing, 1985. Musée des Arts de la Mode, Paris, 1986. Tretyakov Gallery, Moscow, 1986. State Hermitage Museum, St. Petersburg, 1987. Art Gallery, Sydney, 1987. Sezon Museum of Art, Tokyo, 1990. Musée de la Mode, Marseille, 1993.
Publications
Harper's Bazaar, United States, September 1964.
Vogue, France, December 1983.

141
Evening Gown
Fall–Winter 1982
Silk crêpe by Abraham. Rocaille hoop earrings by Goossens. Plastic and stone bracelets by Rieux. Crêpe sandals with pleated bows.
Made to order for the Comtesse de Ribes.
Metropolitan Museum of Art, New York, 1983. Musée des Arts de la Mode, Paris, 1986. Tretyakov Gallery, Moscow, 1986. State Hermitage Museum, St. Petersburg, 1987. Art Gallery, Sydney, 1987. Sezon Museum of Art, Tokyo, 1990. Musée de la Mode, Marseille, 1993.

142
Daytime Ensemble
Fall–Winter 1990
Dress and shawl in cashmere by Abraham. Fox-fur toque and belt by Lemarchand. Suede gloves. Metal pendant earrings. Leather pumps.
Publication
Hola, Spain, January 1, 1990.

143
Evening Ensemble
Spring–Summer 1986
Cardigan, sequin, bugle bead, and rocaille embroidery by Lesage. Dress in silk jersey by Racine. Stud earrings by Roux. Hammered metal ring by Goossens. Rhinestone chains. Satin sandals.
Cardigan made to order for Hélène Rochas.

144
Evening Gown
Fall–Winter 1987
Ostrich feather embroidery by Lemarié. Satin ribbon by Guillemin. Rock crystal and metal pendant earrings. Colored bead, rock crystal, stone, coral, and metal cabochon necklace. Stone and metal ring by Goossens. Satin pumps.

145
Evening Gown
Spring–Summer 1983
Sequin "scales" embroidery with bugle beads, rocaille, and rhinestones by Lesage. Jet and rhinestone cabochon stud earrings by Goossens. Faceted bead, jet, and metal cuffs by Boutron. Rhinestone ankle bracelet by Goossens. Satin sandals with stone cabochons and rhinestones.
Metropolitan Museum of Art, New York, 1983. Palace of Fine Arts, Beijing, 1985. Musée des Arts de la Mode, Paris, 1986. Tretiakov Gallery, 1986. State Hermitage Museum, St. Petersburg, 1987. Art Gallery, Sydney, 1987. Sezon Museum of Art, Tokyo, 1990. Musée de la Mode, Marseille, 1993.

146
Ensemble
Fall–Winter 2000
Cape of rooster feathers by Lemarié. Dress of lacquered panné velvet by Ghioldi. Rhinestone, cabochon, and metal stud earrings. Pumps with satin bows.
Publication
Vogue, France, September 2000.

147
Evening Ensemble
Fall–Winter 1990
Coat with pheasant and vulture feather embroidery by Lemarié. Dress in muslin by Abraham and Bianchini. Pendant earrings. Metal and crystal cuffs. Satin pumps.
Musée de la Mode, Marseille, 1993. Fondation Pierre Bergé–Yves Saint Laurent, Paris, 2006.
Publication
Elle, Germany, March 1992.

FLORA

"I LOVE TREES, FLOWERS. I FOUND THE CLIMATE
OF MY CHILDHOOD IN MARRAKECH, AND
IN TANGIER. VEGETATION IS VERY IMPORTANT
BECAUSE IT BRINGS MUCH SERENITY."

Yves Saint Laurent

The armfuls of flowers and leaves, fleeing the sad destiny of neat flowerbeds composes an elegy to a rich and surprising nature. The bouquets of roses will make dresses of light and air vibrate, à la Jean-Antoine Watteau or Impressionism. In 1999, Laetitia Casta was the incarnation of the mythological bride, the goddess Flora or Botticelli's Venus. Yves Saint Laurent took his summer 1990 collection for a stroll in the Jardin de Guermantes, rendering homage to Marcel Proust, his favorite author.

Musée

Jacqueline

5212

55

Robe du soir long
en piqué noir
jupe brodée de Zinnias
roses, rouges et oranges
veste boutonnée da
le dos et ceinturée
de satin noir

52

2473
Relisia

couronne de roses

Mariée

7446

Laetitia / Colette
68

soutien gorge
de gazar
lurex rose
Gandini
Malvina cil 2
et roses de
art hemarie

7446 bis Colette
Culotte idem
et roses de
art hemarie

1 rose au poignet

1 rose à
la cheville
gauche
Sandales
rose pâle
satin gandini
Morgan 78

Fait le 1411
Fait le 1411

152_2

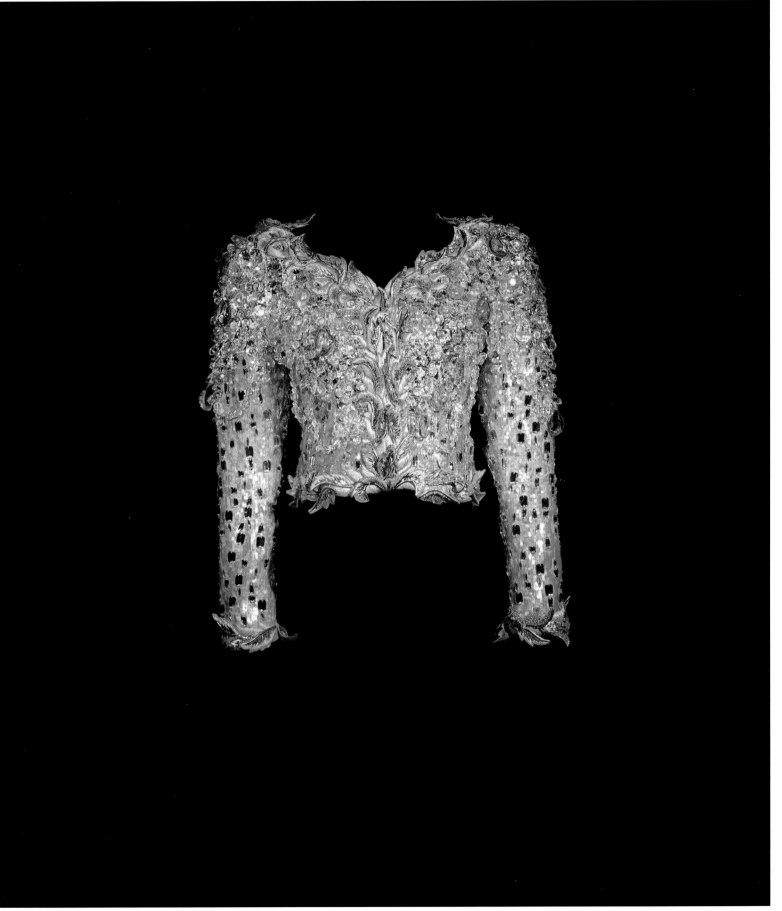

154_1

113

Or, cristal et
bleu
glacier

Sandales
Satin
Bleu ciel
bracelet
diamants

collants
clairs

Musée 5295 x
Georges / Edna
Arianne
Veste brodée Lesage
(fond organza satin blc
Abraham 8008/100

5295 bis - Robe de satin
blanc - baby -
Abraham 3889/Blc1

B.O chute de perles blanches
et perles de verre sur métal or
couvrette de perles - Cj4

1 ceinture flots de rangs de
perle blanche avec pépites or
fermée par plaque de perle et
or avec chute devant de plusieurs
rangs.

1 bague fleur de diamants
miroir.

Ch. 101.

154_2

234

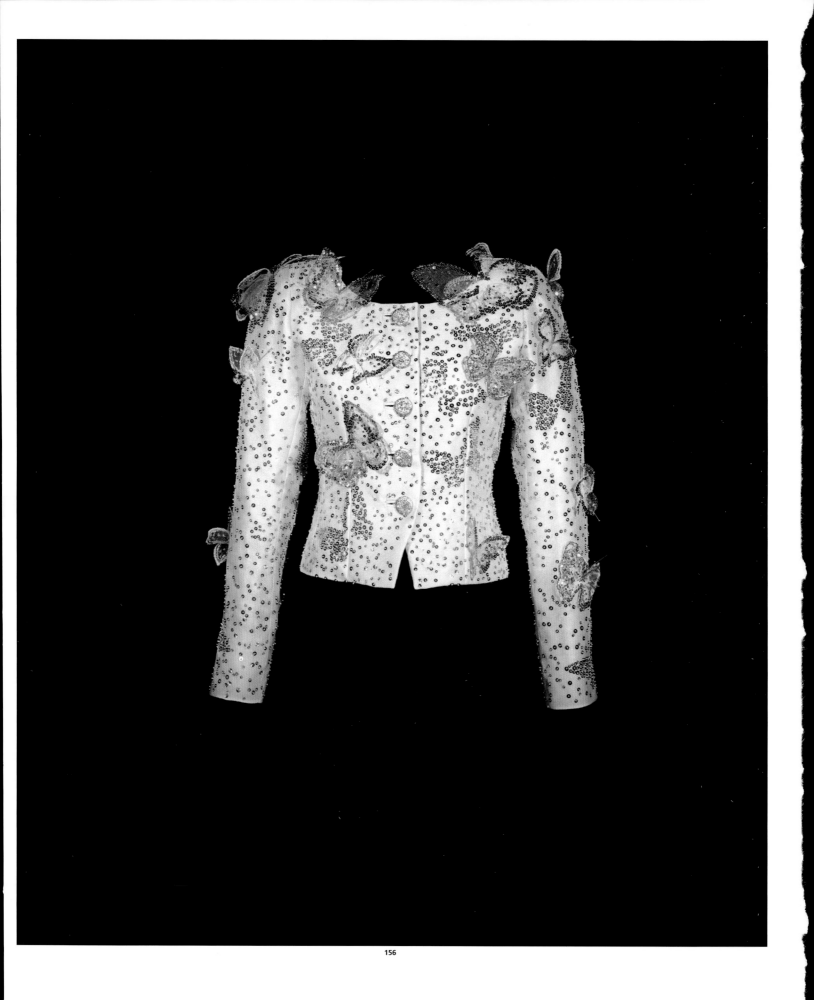

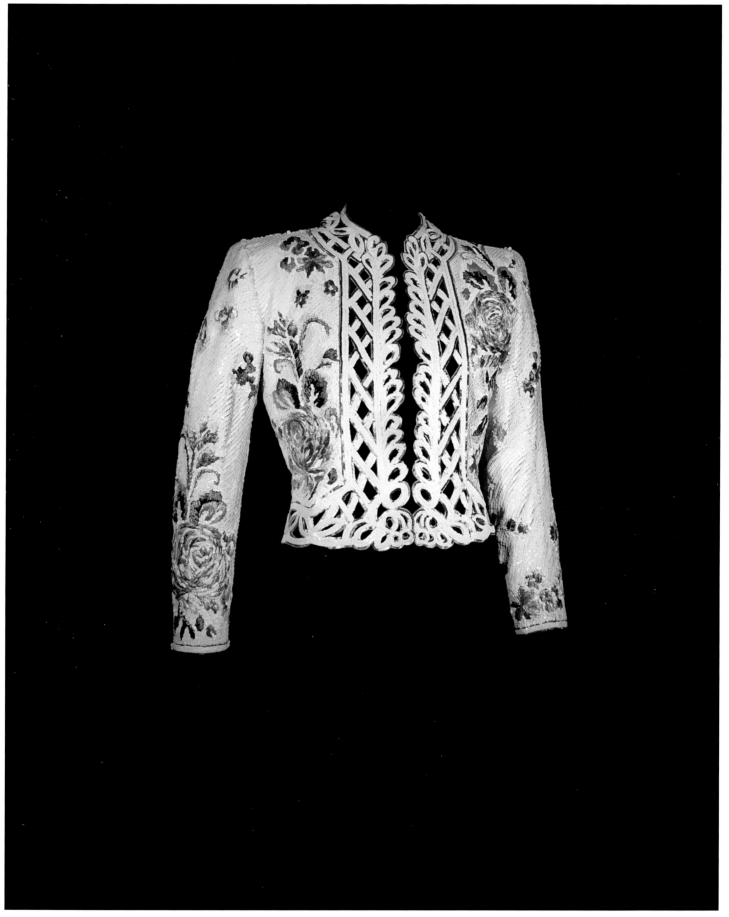

"MAKING THE STATIC THINGS MOVE ON THE
BODY OF A WOMAN."

Yves Saint Laurent, *Paris Match,* France, February 12, 1988.

148_1, 148_2
Evening Gown in Tribute to Christian Dior
Spring–Summer 1990
Chine taffeta by Abraham. Roses by Lemarié. Metal and glass bead pendant earrings. Satin pumps.

149
Cocktail Dress in Tribute to Marcel Proust
Spring–Summer 1990
Organdie by Abraham. Ceramic, metal, glass, and stone pendant earrings. Enamel and rhinestone metal ring. Rock crystal and metal ring. Flower coiffure. Satin strap sandals.

150
Evening Gown
Spring–Summer 1962
Piqué cotton by Moreau. Silk and rocaille embroidery by Rébé. Plastic stud earrings. Jet and rhinestone bracelet. Satin gloves and sandals.
Donated by the Comtesse de Ribes.
Metropolitan Museum of Art, New York, 1983.

151
Full-Length Dress
Spring–Summer 1986
Chine taffeta by Abraham. "Star" ear studs in metal and rhinestone by Goossens. Metal and cabochon crystal and rhinestone ring by Caillol. Metal, pearl, and rhinestone bracelet by Sabbagh. Satin sandals.
Musée des Arts de la Mode, Paris, 1986. Tretyakov Gallery, Moscow, 1986. State Hermitage Museum, St. Petersburg, 1987. Art Gallery, Sydney, 1987. Sezon Museum of Art, Tokyo, 1990.

152_1, 152_2
Bridal Gown
Spring–Summer 1999
Bridal wreath, bracelet, and ankle bracelet of roses and leaves by Lemarié. Train in silk gazar by Gandini. Crepe sandals.
Publication
Le Point, France, January 1999.

153
Evening Gown
Spring–Summer 1997
Flower and leaf sequin, stone, and organza embroidery by Lesage. Satin ribbon by Guillemin. Metal, stone, and rhinestone earrings by Boutron. Satin sandals.

154_1, 154_2
Evening Jacket in Tribute to Ma Maison
Spring–Summer 1990
Sequin, plastic, and faceted glass cabochon embroidery of paillettes by Lesage.
Sezon Museum of Art, Tokyo, 1990.
Publication
L'Officiel, France, March 1, 1990.

155
Evening Jacket
Spring–Summer 1991
"Flower" embroidery in colored beads. Silk by Lanel.

156
Evening Jacket
Spring–Summer 1995
"Butterfly" tulle embroidery. Sequins and stones by Montex.
Publication
Harper's Bazaar, Italy, March 1995.

157
Evening Jacket
Spring–Summer 1992
Sequin and raffia "flower" embroidery by Lesage.
Publications
Vogue, France, March 1992.
Harper's Bazaar, Italy, March 1992.

C24	PE 1994 → AH 1994
C23	AH 1993 → PE 1994
C22	AH 1992 → PE 1993
C21	PE 1992 → AH 1992
C20	AH 1991 → PE 1992
C19	AH 1991

BIOG-
RAPHY

1936

Yves Saint Laurent was born on August 1 in Oran, Algeria, where he spent all his childhood and graduated from school (fig. 1–2). He then left Oran for Paris.

1953

At the age of seventeen, he showed his drawings to Michel de Brunhoff, director of *Vogue,* who kept several of them for use in his magazine.

1954

After studying at a couture school, he won first prize in a competition to design a cocktail dress, organized by the Wool Secretariat.

Michel de Brunhoff then introduced him to Christian Dior, who hired him. He eventually became Dior's collaborator until Dior's death in 1957.

1958

Saint Laurent meets Pierre Bergé. Yves Saint Laurent confides: "It was an extraordinary meeting. He had everything that I didn't have. In the event, he was very important for me. Without him, I would never have known what I have known. He freed me from my shyness. His strength was something important for me. I could lean on him when I was tired out. Pierre Bergé is the story of my life."

He wins the Neiman Marcus Oscar.

In January, he presents his first collection at Dior. *Trapeze* is a howling success. From one day to the next, Yves Saint Laurent becomes more and more famous (fig. 3).

From 1958 through 1960, Yves Saint Laurent creates six collections at Dior, where he continues to work. "Monsieur Dior taught me the essential basics of this profession, as well as its dignity," he acknowledged.

3

1

2

1959

For the first time, Yves Saint Laurent designs costumes for the theater (*Cyrano de Bergerac*, the ballet by Roland Petit); he will continue to pursue this activity successfully throughout his career.

1961

Unable to return to Dior after the brief interruption of his work due to the army draft, he announces his intention to open his own couture house. In September, Yves Saint Laurent opens his couture house with Pierre Bergé in a two-room apartment on rue La Boétie, in Paris. He gets financial support from the American J. Mack Robinson who, thanks to his dynamism and unshakeable confidence in the talent of the young designer, is instantly enthusiastic about the project.

In December, Yves Saint Laurent designs the first dress in his own name, for Mme. Arturo Lopez-Willshaw.

The graphic designer Adolphe Mouron Cassandre creates the Yves Saint Laurent logo (fig. 4).

1962

On January 29, Yves Saint Laurent presents his first collection, which *Life* magazine (fig. 5) describes as "the best collection of suits designed since Chanel." His offerings include a daring adaptation of a famous French garment, the *caban* (sailor's jacket), as well as the Norman blouse.

1964

Still very busy designing for the theater, he designs the costumes for *The Marriage of Figaro* and *Il faut passer par les nuages* (*You Have to Go Via the Clouds*) by the Renaud-Barrault company.

1965

He presents his famous "Mondrian" dress, the first homage inspired by a painter. Diana Vreeland summarizes the collection with enthusiasm: "It is . . . finished, subtle, ravishing, French, and very feminine."

1966

The Spring-Summer collection shows "sailor suits," one of Yves Saint Laurent's favorite themes: pantsuit, sailor's jacket, and striped T-shirt dress.

The first tuxedo for women revolutionizes fashion (fig. 6).

Inspired by the contemporary trends in art—and by Andy Warhol in particular—he launches his "Pop Art" dresses (fig. 7).

On September 26, Yves Saint Laurent opens his first ready-to-wear boutique, Saint Laurent Rive Gauche, on the rue de Tournon, in Paris's sixth arrondissement (the Latin Quarter).

1967

Saint Laurent's first major homage to Africa with a collection that is surprising in its creativity (fig. 8).

This is the year of the pantsuit.

The designer dresses Catherine Deneuve in Luis Buñuel's movie *Belle de jour*.

1968

Saint Laurent designs the "Transparencies" jumpsuit and his first safari suit (fig 9–10).

6   9

4

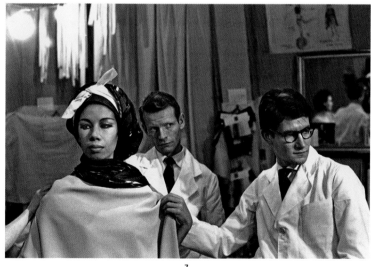

7

5

1969

Saint Laurent collaborates with the artist Claude Lalanne (fig. 11).

1971

Yves Saint Laurent presents *The Fourties* collection, as a reaction to the new fashion trends. It features square shoulders, bouffant sleeves, and platform heels, as well as the famous short, green fox-fur jacket. "I was inspired by Paloma Picasso, when I saw her one day coming to an event in a turban, platform shoes, one of her mother's 1940s dresses, and outrageously made up. She made an extreme impression on me.

Yves Saint Laurent poses in the nude for the photographer Jean-Loup Sieff (fig. 12).

1972

Andy Warhol paints four portraits of Yves Saint Laurent.

1974

In July, the couture house moves to 5, avenue Marceau, in Paris's upmarket sixteenth arrondissement. The building is a late-nineteenth-century mansion decorated in the style of that period.

1976

Triumph of the *Russian* collection (fig. 13). "Everything was designed in color, the smallest detail, shoes, hats. . . . It was the first time I had worked like this, in a huge spurt of creativity. This collection was created at a time when people were saying that haute couture was finished. And yet it still had something to say. Inspired by the *ballets russes* and Verdi's operas for the evening wear. I think it was the greatest success I ever had."

1977

Les Chinoises collection (fig. 14) and launch of the new perfume "Opium."

1978

Yves Saint Laurent designs the sets and costumes for *The Two-Headed Eagle* by Jean Cocteau at the Théâtre de l'Athénée.

1979

Collection in homage to Pablo Picasso and Serge Diaghilev.

11

12

8   **10**

1981

Yves Saint Laurent creates Marguerite Yourcenar's uniform for her entry into the Académie française (fig. 15).

Collection in homage to Matisse.

1983

The Metropolitan Museum of Art in New York, under the direction of Diana Vreeland, organizes a major retrospective: "Yves Saint Laurent—25 Years of Design." It is the first time that a tribute of such importance has been dedicated to a living fashion designer (fig. 16).

1985

Yves Saint Laurent is invited to the Palace of Fine Arts in Beijing to present a retrospective entitled: "Yves Saint Laurent, 1958–1985" (fig. 17).

On March 12, François Mitterrand, President of the French Republic, decorates him with the insignia of a Chevalier of the Légion d'honneur at the Élysée Palace.

On October 23, Yves Saint Laurent receives an Oscar from La Mode.

1986

For its reopening, the Musée des Arts et de la mode de Paris presents a tribute to Yves Saint Laurent entitled: "28 years of creation."

In December, the "Yves Saint Laurent" exhibition is held at the Tretiakov Gallery in Moscow.

1987

In February, the "Yves Saint Laurent" exhibition is held at the Ermitage Museum in St. Petersburg.

1988

Homage to Vincent van Gogh with "Irises" and "Sunflowers." These are the two most expensive jackets created by Yves Saint Laurent.

1990

In November and December, the Sezon Museum of Art in Tokyo organizes a retrospective entitled "Yves Saint Laurent 1958–1990," as well as an exhibition of his theater designs and an exhibition of fashion photography.

13

14

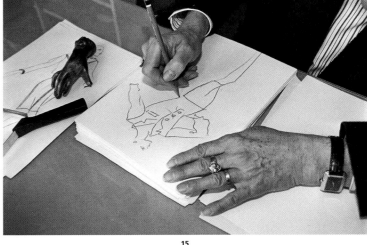

15

16

17

1998

Celebration of forty years of creation by Yves Saint Laurent.

Yves Saint Laurent organizes the spectacle at the Soccer World Cup Final. Three hundred models parade for 80,000 spectators and more than two billion television viewers (fig. 18).

Yves Saint Laurent and Pierre Bergé sponsor a wing in their names dedicated to French painting at the National Gallery in London.

1999

On June 2, in New York, the Council of Fashion Designers of America awards Yves Saint Laurent with a Lifetime Achievement Award.

2001

On March 24, Yves Saint Laurent receives the Rosa d'Oro in Palermo.

2002

On January 7, the haute couture house organizes a press conference during which Yves Saint Laurent announces his wish to retire from his profession as couturier.

On January 22, the last retrospective fashion parade is held at the Centre Georges-Pompidou, retracing his forty years of creation before a host of famous personalities, and he presents his last Spring-Summer collection for 2002 (fig. 19–20).

On October 31, the haute couture house closes.

On December 5, the Fondation Pierre Bergé–Yves Saint Laurent is recognized as being of public utility by a decree published in the *Journal officiel*.

On December 31, they buy the mansion at 5, avenue Marceau, which will become the headquarters of the foundation (fig. 21–22).

From now on, Yves Saint Laurent dedicates his activities and exhibitions to the foundation. The whole of the Saint Laurent heritage, dating back to 1962, is preserved here, consisting of 5,000 garments, 15,000 accessories, and thousands of sketches.

2004

On March 10, the foundation opens its doors to the public with the exhibition entitled "Yves Saint Laurent—Dialogue with Art." Forty-two models and five of the master's toiles are evidence of the close relations between Yves Saint Laurent and art (fig. 23–24).

21

23

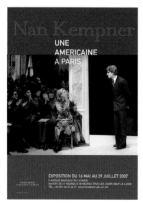

24

19

20

18

22

APPEN-DIXES

CHRONOLOGICAL INDEX OF DESIGNS

1958
Spring–Summer
"Trapeze" Dress, 32

1962
Spring–Summer
Daytime Ensemble, 61, 62
Evening Gown, 222
Fall–Winter
Evening Ensemble, 62
Formal Dress, 33

1963
Fall–Winter
Daytime Ensemble, 68

1964
Spring–Summer
Cocktail Dress, 34
Fall–Winter
Evening Ensemble, 209

1965
Fall–Winter
Bridal Gown, 50
Cocktail Dress (Tribute to P. Mondrian), 169, 171
Cocktail Dress (Tribute to S. Poliakoff), 170
Evening Gown, 41

1966
Spring–Summer
Cocktail Dress, 63
"Op Art" Suit, 152
Fall–Winter
Cocktail Dress (Tribute to T. Wesselmann), 171
Day Dress, 76
Full-Length Evening Gown (Tribute to T. Wesselmann), 172–73
Premier Tuxedo, 85

1967
Spring–Summer
"Bambara" Dress, 111
Evening Gown, 105–7, 109, 113
Pantsuit, 56
Skirtsuit, 57
"Tropical" Dress, 109, 110
Fall–Winter
Evening Ensemble, 86
Skirtsuit, 63
Special Commission
"Belle de Jour" Dress, 82

1968
Spring–Summer
Tuxedo, 92
July (Special commission by *Vogue*)
Daytime Ensemble, 65
Fall–Winter
Evening Gown, 87, 151
Evening Ensemble, 77

1969
Spring–Summer
Cocktail Dress, 153
Full-Length Evening Gown, 141
Fall–Winter
Evening Gown, 178, 179
Evening Ensemble, 98, 134
Jumpsuit, 66

1970
Spring–Summer
Evening Ensemble, 142
Tuxedo, 88
Fall–Winter
Bridal Gown, 180
Day Dress, 69
Evening Gown, 41
Evening Ensemble, 118

1971
Spring–Summer
Day Dress, 79
Daytime Ensemble, 70
Evening Coat, 75
Evening Gown, 81
Silk Coat, 78

1973
Fall–Winter
Evening Ensemble, 90

1975
Fall–Winter
Skirtsuit, 58

1976
Fall–Winter
Daytime Ensemble, 126, 127
Evening Gown, 129, 133
Evening Ensemble, 128, 130, 131

1977
Spring–Summer
Cocktail Ensemble, 122
Evening Gown, 120
Evening Ensemble, 121
Fall–Winter
Evening Ensemble, 49, 115, 116
"Opium" Evening Ensemble, 117

1978
Spring–Summer
Pantsuit, 58
Fall–Winter
Evening Ensemble, 193

1979
Spring–Summer
Pantsuit, 203
Fall–Winter
Toreador Costume, 123
Cocktail Dress (Tribute to P. Picasso), 175
Evening Gown, 124, 153
Evening Ensembles (Tribute to P. Picasso), 176–77

1980
Spring–Summer
Evening Gown, 80
Fall–Winter
Bridal Gown (Tribute to W. Shakespeare), 198
Evening Gown, 162
Evening Gown (Tribute to H. Matisse), 181
Evening Ensemble (Tribute to G. Apollinaire), 196
Evening Ensemble (Tribute to L. Aragon), 196
Evening Ensemble (Tribute to J. Cocteau), 194–95

1981
Fall–Winter
Evening Gown, 49, 80
Evening Gown (Tribute to H. Matisse), 182
Evening Ensemble (Tribute to H. Matisse), 183
Evening Suit, 135

1982
Fall–Winter
Cocktail Dress, 35
Evening Gown, 210

1983
Spring–Summer
Evening Gown, 42, 214
Fall–Winter
Evening Gown, 202

1984
Fall–Winter
Evening Ensemble, 72, 155, 163

1985
Spring–Summer
Evening Gown, 43

1986
Spring–Summer
Evening Ensemble, 212
Full-Length Dress, 223
Fall–Winter
Evening Gown, 136

1987
Spring–Summer
Evening Gown, 143
Fall–Winter
Evening Gown, 213

1988
Spring–Summer
Evening Gown (Tribute to G. Braque), 186, 187
Evening Ensemble, 99
Evening Ensembles (Tribute to G. Braque), 188, 190
Irises Ensemble (Tribute to V. Van Gogh), 184
Sunflowers Ensemble (Tribute to V. Van Gogh), 185
Fall–Winter
Bridal Gown, 36
Daytime Ensemble, 59

1989
Spring–Summer
Cocktail Ensemble, 145
Evening Ensemble, 100–1
Fall–Winter
Daytime Ensemble, 144

1990
Spring–Summer
Cocktail Dress (Tribute to M. Proust), 221
Evening Gown (Tribute to C. Dior), 219–20
Evening Gown (Tribute to M. Monroe), 201
Evening Jacket (Tribute to Ma Maison), 229, 234
Evening Tunic (Tribute to Zizi Jeanmaire), 44–45
Fall–Winter
Daytime Ensemble, 211
Evening Gown, 43, 164
Evening Ensemble, 216

1991
Spring–Summer
Evening Gown, 49
Evening Ensemble (Tribute to L. Bakst), 102
Evening Jacket, 230
Fall–Winter
Evening Gown, 80, 137
Tuxedo, 91

1992
Spring–Summer
Cocktail Dress, 156
Evening Jacket, 232
Fall–Winter
Evening Ensemble, 146

1993
Fall–Winter
Evening Gown, 46, 47
Tuxedo (Tribute to O. Wilde), 197

1994
Fall–Winter
Evening Ensemble, 119

1995
Spring–Summer
Evening Jacket, 231
Fall–Winter
Trench Coat, 67

1996
Fall–Winter
Tuxedo, 37

1997
Spring–Summer
Evening Gown, 227
Fall–Winter
Evening Gown, 38, 165
Evening Gown "Holbein," 166

1998
Fall–Winter
Evening Gown, 204

1999
Spring–Summer
Bridal Gown, 224–25
Fall–Winter
Evening Gown, 38
Pantsuit, 60
Tuxedo, 89

2000
Fall–Winter
Bridal Gown (Tribute to A. Renoir), 189
Daytime Ensemble, 71, 125
Ensemble, 215
Evening Gown, 49
Evening Ensemble, 147

2001
Spring–Summer
Evening Ensemble, 205
Full-Length Evening Gown, 206

2002
Spring–Summer
Evening Ensemble, 148

Fabrics
Abraham, Allaman, Aquaviva, Besson, Bianchini, Brivet, Buche, Bucol, Carlatto, Chatillon, Clerici, Daure, Dormeuil, Fournier, Gandini, Garigue, Ghioldi, Guillaud, Helsa, Holland & Sherry, Hurel, Leleu, Léonard, Lesur, Marescot, Moreau, Pennel, Perceval, Pétillault, Prud'homme, Racine, Raimon, Rodier, Rodolphe Simon, Saris, Schlaepfer, Sophie, Staron, Taroni

Leather and skins
Cuvreau, Poulain, Sonia

Passementerie (trimmings)
Denez, Leroux, Merieux, Trégal

Knitting
Closset, Michel Paris

Furriers
Garande, Lavabre-Cadet, Pelletier

Ribbons
Guillemin

Embroidery
Brossin de Méré, Lanel, Lesage, Lisbeth, Malhia, Mesrine, Montex, Rébé

Plumassiers (feather working)
Barbier, Lemarié

Paruriers (jewel sewing)
Fromentin, Nina Wood

Jewelry
Baschet, Boutron, Caillol, Courlande, Denez, Goossens, Labeyre, Péral, Rieux, Roux, Sabbagh

Shoes
Roger Vivier

Hairstyling
Alexandre de Paris

Belts
Hamon, Lemarchand

Fondation
Pierre Bergé–Yves Saint Laurent

This book is a companion volume to the
retrospective Yves Saint Laurent, organized
and produced by the Montreal Museum of
Fine Arts and the Fine Arts Museums of San
Francisco in collaboration with the
Fondation Pierre Bergé–Yves Saint Laurent.

Exhibition curators:
Florence Müller
Jill D'Alessandro
Diane Charbonneau

Montreal:
May 29 through September 28, 2008

San Francisco:
November 1, 2008, through March 1, 2009

Photographs:
Alexandre Guirkinger
All drawings were provided by the
Fondation Pierre Bergé–Yves Saint Laurent

Designer:
Philippe Apeloig
Design assistant:
Elamine Maecha

For the English-language edition:

Essays and captions translated from the
French by Josephine Bacon

Project Manager:
Magali Veillon
Editor:
Jon Cipriaso
Designer:
Shawn Dahl
Production Manager:
Jules Thomson

Library of Congress Cataloging-in-Publication
Data

Berge, Pierre.
   Yves Saint Laurent / Pierre Berge.
        p. cm.
   ISBN 978-0-8109-7120-2
   1. Saint Laurent, Yves. 2. Fashion
designers—France—Biography. I. Title.

TT505.S24B48 2008
746.9'2092—dc22

                      2008004808

Printed and bound in Italy
10 9 8 7 6 5 4 3 2

Abrams books are available at special
discounts when purchased in quantity
for premiums and promotions as well
as fundraising or educational use.
Special editions can also be created to
specification. For details, contact
specialmarkets@hnabooks.com or the
address below.

HNA ▪▪▪▪▪
harry n. abrams, inc.
a subsidiary of La Martinière Groupe

115 West 18th Street
New York, NY 10011
www.hnabooks.com

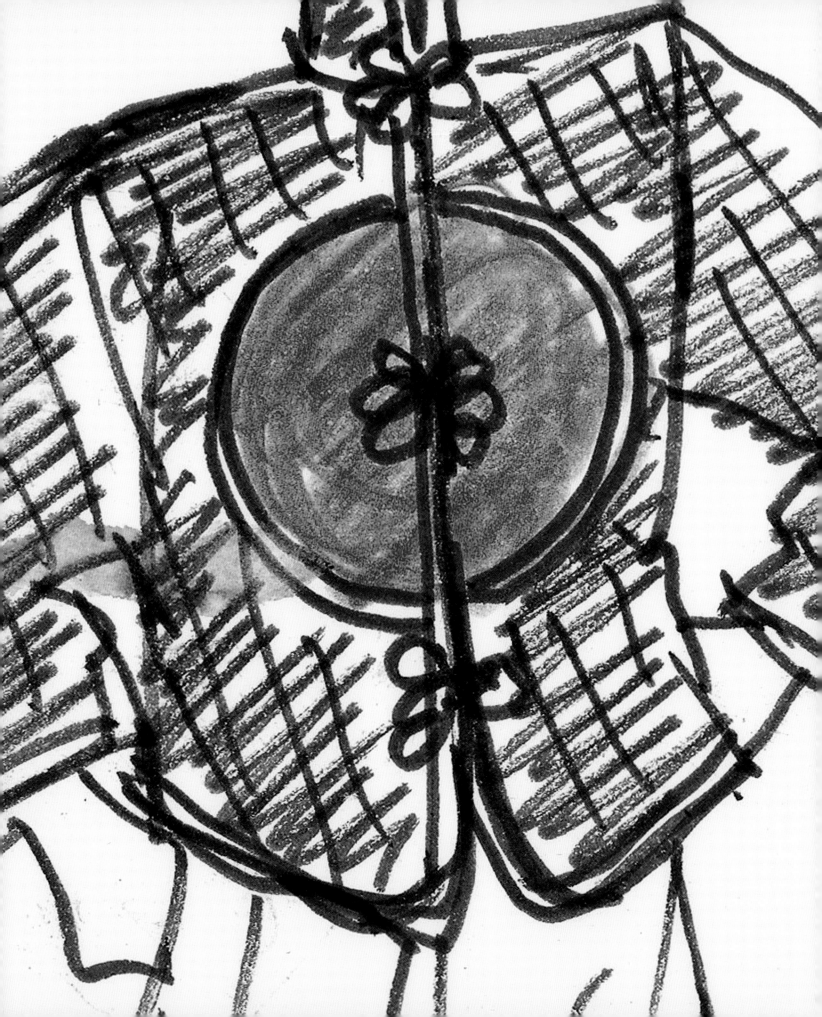

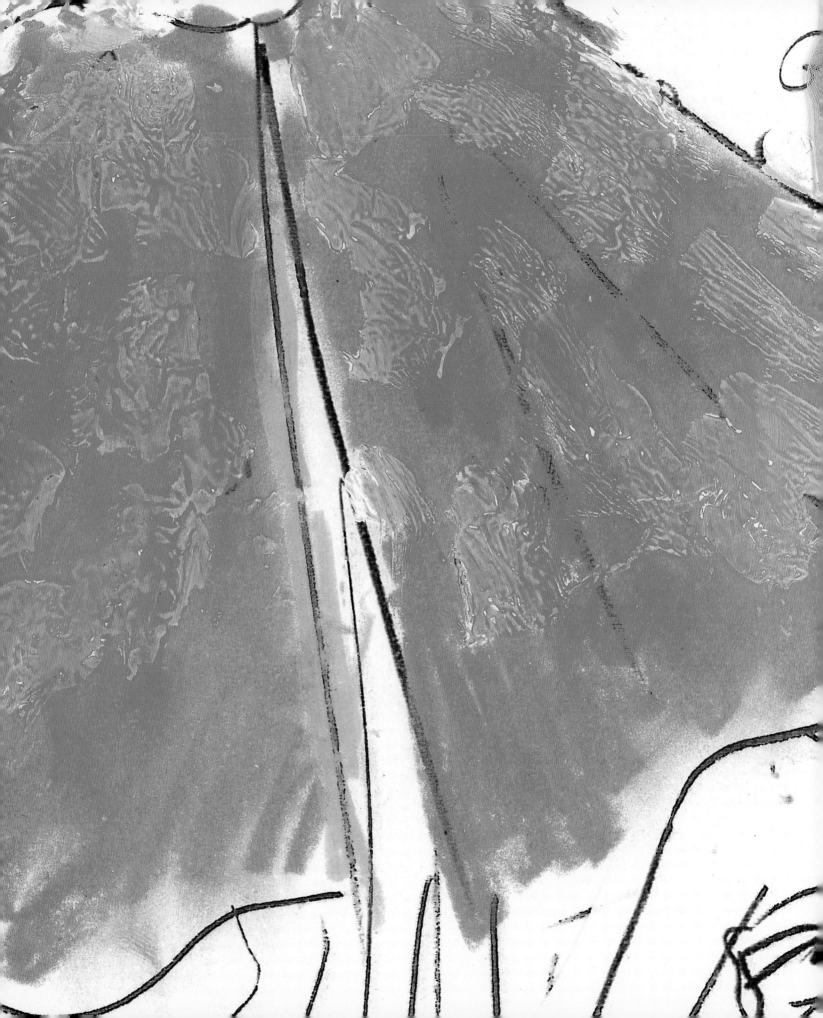